THE
ILLUMINATI
DESTRUCTION OF AMERICA

"None Are More Hopelessly Enslaved
Than Those Who Falsely Believe They Are Free!"
- Johann von Goethe

This publication constitutes only the communication of information in accordance with the rights of Freedom of Speech and Freedom of the Press, as guaranteed by the First Amendment to the Constitution of the United States of America. It does not challenge or threaten the authority of any legitimate government, nor advocate nonpayment of legitimate taxes.

This publication is designed to provide accurate and authoritative information with regard to the subject matter covered. It does not necessarily reflect the opinions of its publishers, advertisers, promoters or distributors. It is sold and distributed only with the understanding that the publisher is not engaged in rendering legal, accounting, or other manner of professional advice. If legal advice or other expert professional assistance is required, the services of a competent professional person or company should be sought.

Dear Friend and Associate,

I want to thank you very much for purchasing this information. help us all to reclaim our Rights, our Freedoms, and our Privacy... In other words, to live our lives as we wish, unrestricted by false regulations thrust upon us by tyrants, who aspire to become wealthy masters over us, their eternal servants!

This report is dedicated to assisting all of us - not only citizens of the United States, but of every country in the world -to increase our personal freedom by realizing that we are the masters of our own fate. We do not have to depend on other humans to "grant" us our freedom, our rights, our privacy, and our very dignity... Those things are already *ours!* We need only recognize this truth... which is what this report is all about!

Everybody has his or her own story, I guess. For me it all began with a very painful personal experience of just a couple of short years ago... I was forced to declare bankruptcy, and as a result, I started taking a closer look at the entire economic system, which had accelerated - if not actually *caused* - my financial demise.

My first "revelation" was that 'money' as we know it, is worth only a small fraction of what it was worth less than two generations ago! Since 'money' - in one form or another - has been around for all of recorded history without evidence of such drastic changes on a global scale, I began to dig deeper to find out what was *really* going on!

As a result of trying to find out what happened to our money, I kept encountering an even bigger and much more important question: "What happened to our Freedom?" Most of us grudgingly acknowledge that our privacy is practically a thing of the past... and more and more people are becoming aware that most of our rights guaranteed by the Constitution have also been relinquished. Why? I became determined to get to the bottom of it!

THE BEGINNING

The idea of world domination is not new. All history is filled with dictators and groups of people who tried to conquer and enslave others: Alexander the Great; the Roman Empire; Attila the Hun; the Holy Roman Empire; the Ottoman Empire, etc. But all of these early attempts to conquer the world were done by individuals or groups working alone and using great speed and brute force to accomplish their goals. The people the conquered were very painfully aware of what had happened to them, and bitterly hated their enslavers, so in time they always rose up against their conquerors to overthrow them. As they say, History repeats itself... until recently.

A little over 200 years ago, there began a traceable sequence of events never before seen in all of recorded history! Like a tiny pebble dropped into a pond, causing ripples to spread across the entire surface of the water, this pattern of events began with a very small seed of an idea which has grown into ever-widening circles. But unlike the pebble's ripples, which slowly loose their force and impact, the circles of influence spawned by this small seed of an idea have grown not only in size, but also in strength and power until now they are the force and impact behind all the major governments in the entire world!

This small seed of an idea began with the age-old desire of men to rule the world - but this time there was to be a difference. No more marauding armies. No despotic dictators. No chains or torture. Nothing to give the conquered masses any clear idea of who the enemy was - or that an enemy even *existed!* Just a meticulously planned and subtly implemented plot to enslave the entire planet into a worldwide dictatorship, a "New World Order." Instead of open aggression and invading troops which are easily recognized and branded as 'the enemy" 9 the enslavement of all the world's population was to be done secretly, behind closed doors, in clandestine meetings... and not by some lone dictator, but by a closed club of "elitists" whose goal was/is world domination. 'Their insidious plan has almost reached it's final, frightening conclusion, for they hope to have their "New World Order" of global dominance in full control by the year 2000...

About now you're probably wondering, "But what do you mean by 'no more marauding armies'? In the last 200 years, the world has seen more insurrections, revolutions, invasions, and other wars than all the rest of recorded history combined!" And you would be right! The difference is that in this most recent period of history, *every major military conflict - and most minor ones as well - have been carefully planned, implemented and orchestrated by this elitist group, whom we shall call the "international banking conspirators'!*

Your next thought will very likely be (like mine was), "An international conspiracy? Give me a break! If our own Congress can't even agree on anything, how could people from numerous cultures and backgrounds possibly conspire together to create an4binz, let alone a 'one world government!"

Good point! And one that is counted on by the conspirators You see, 1, too firmly believed that there never was and never could be anything so vast and well-organized as an international conspiracy of this magnitude... a conspiracy that has gone (for the most part) completely undetected by its victims for so long a time.

In school (which is largely controlled by these monsters - as you will soon see) we are taught an "accidental" version of history. This "accidental' perspective takes the view that most things 'just happen" in an unplanned, disorganized or chaotic manner. For example, World War I started because Archduke Ferdinand was assassinated. Period. It "just happened." The Federal Reserve was created to prevent massive boom-bust cycles in the economy. Period. The boom-bust cycles "just happened." The last 6 major military operations Of the US (Korea, Vietnam, Iraq, Somalia, Haiti and Bosnia) have all been under the 'authority' of the United Nations in the name of 'international cooperation and global harmony.' There was no particular reason for the UN having control; it was just a "nice" way of doing things. In other words, 'It just happened." Period.

But if you look a little closer - if you dig a little deeper - you might start to ask yourself, "Who had a motive? Who killed the Archduke, why did they do it, and who benefited?" Or, 'Who or what caused the massive boom-bust cycles in the economy before the Federal Reserve was created, and who benefited from its creation?" And more recently, "Why has the US ceded some of its sovereignty (without the consent of the citizens) to the UN? How much power rightfully belonging to the 'government of the people by the people, and for the people' has been given without the consent 'of the people' to the UN?" "Who benefits by this unauthorized transition of power (and who loses)?"

When you ask these probing questions, and the answers all point to the international banking cartel (hereafter referred to as "conspirators" or "international banking conspiracy"), you can come to no other conclusion that there was, and *still* is, an international conspiracy of monstrous proportions, designed to destroy all remaining vestiges of individual freedom and liberty, and plunge the entire planet into despotic and demonic dictatorship, far more terrifying than anything the world has ever seen!

Franklin D. Roosevelt (who was one of the conspiracy insiders, as we will soon see) said it best: "In politics nothing happens by accident. If it happened, you can bet it was *planned* that way! "...Then why do most of us scoff at the very idea of a conspiracy? We flatly refuse to believe (as I did) that such an insidious and all-encompassing plot could have been so secretly and meticulously woven against us, completely without our knowledge.

It really is hard to believe the sheer magnitude and intricacy of the web of deceit, fraud and outright lies that has been carefully woven around us! But the main reason most people refuse to believe that a conspiracy even exists, is that we *have all been brainwashed into believing that such a thing could never happen!* G. Edward Griffin, author of *The Creature From Jekyll Island* (an in-depth expose of the Federal Reserve), puts it this way: "The reason it [a conspiracy] is hard to accept is that we have been conditioned [by the conspiracy controlled media and education system] to laugh at conspiracy theories, and few people will risk public ridicule by advocating them. On the other hand, to endorse the accidental view is absurd. Almost all of history is an unbroken trail of one conspiracy after another. Conspiracies are the norm not the exception.' Or as author Arthur Edward Waite observed, "Beneath the broad tide of human history there flow the stealthy undercurrents of the secret societies, which frequently determine in the depths the changes that take place on the surface."

THE 'ILLUMINATI'

'So you see... the world is governed by very different personages from what is imagined by those who are not behind the scenes. '- Benjamin Disraeli

The term "New World Order" was the motto of the secret society of the "Illuminati" (or "the Enlightened Ones"), which was formed in 1776 by Adam Weishaupt, a Jesuit priest and professor of Canon Law (law of the Church) at Ingoistadt University in Bavaria (a part of southeast Germany, near the Czechoslovakian border). He founded the Illuminati largely in retaliation to the order by Pope Clement XIV to "annul and extinguish the Jesuits," because of their political activism.

By the way, the symbol of the Illuminati (adopted from the Free Masons) was a pyramid, with an "all-seeing eye" at the top (the historical symbol of the Egyptian god Osiris - the dark god, Prince of the dead). This symbol was intended to signify the few enlightened' (intelligentsia) people at the top in a position of power over and supported by the mass of followers (slaves) which comprised the base of the pyramid. At the bottom of the base appeared the number " 1776", which is the year of the founding of the order, and also coincidentally (or *not.),* the year of the American Declaration of Independence. Above the pyramid, in Latin, are the words "Annuit Coeptis", which means, "Our enterprise (conspiracy) has been crowned with success." Below the pyramid, also in Latin, are the words "Novus Ordo Seclorum," meaning "New Order of Things,' or "New World Order."

(As an interesting aside, Adam Weishaupt founded the order of the Illuminati on May lst, 1776... This is why May lst has always been the international "Red' holiday - honoring the birthday of the movement dedicated to the establishment of a global dictatorship, which has become known as the "New World Order", after their own motto!)

I'm sure this symbol is very familiar to you, because it appears on the back of every one 'dollar'' Federal Reserve Note! Of course the next big question is "Why is it on our money?" To answer that question, let's resume our story...

The Illuminati grew quickly, seeking out the "cream of the crop" in European society - the wealthy and well-educated upper class and intellectuals. Although they were among Europe's "finest", they were still below the level of rulers. They were close to "power", but close were not good enough! They truly believed that they were superior to the ruling class, and thus more qualified to rule... In other words, they wanted the power for themselves. Convinced that the 11 Illuminati would soon rule the world, they began to work passionately toward that day when they would become members of the new ruling class.

The philosophy of the Illuminati was that man was not responsible for his actions, society was - and therefore society should be punished for the acts of criminals. They also believed that only an all powerful government of superior people (such as themselves) could properly control society, and make sure that it was "right" - according to the way they believed things "should be".

The 'Secret Plan' of the Illuminati - To achieve this goal of world domination, the Illuminati established a plan that called for total destruction from within (in other words, by infiltration, not insurrection) of all religion, governments, and other previously existing human institutions. They would accomplish this by abolishing: the family as we know it; all religions; all forms of government; all private property and inheritance; patriotism and nationalism and all other forms of individual and national sovereignty. Out of the chaos, anarchy, suffering, and confusion, the Illuminati would establish their new world order.

(Note: Destroy and/or infiltrate then corrupt all previously existing establishments that provided social purpose and stability)

The work of the Illuminati laid the very foundation for modern spying and espionage techniques. By the nature of their quest, they relied on deceit and concealment as the most effective weapons in their struggle to achieve world domination. Exposure and Truth meant Death! Weishaupt knew this only too well! In his own words: "The great strength of our order lies in its concealment. Let it never appear in any place in its own name, but always covered by another name and another occupation."

The order of the Illuminati continued to grow in power and influence, and with an ever-increasing reach into the innermost circles of European governments. Much of the credit for the spread of the Illuminati doctrine is attributed to a single, ambitious banker from Frankfurt, Germany - Amschel Moses Bauer.

Amschel, who later changed his last name to Rothschild (loosely translated to mean "Red Shield"), started a goldsmith shop, a fractional reserve bank, and several smuggling operations by 1743 (when he was barely more than 20 years old!). He began accumulating considerable wealth by lending money to governments.

Experiencing first hand the incredible power that money can wield, Amschel became fascinated with power for its own sake, and the accumulation of more and more of it. He was an avid student of the secret societies of the day which sought global power: the Rosicrucians ("Red Cross Society"); the Free Masons, who are actually credited with originating the Illuminati symbol of the pyramid (representing the unfinished work of the Free Masons), topped by the brightly shining, all-seeing eye of the Illuminati (meaning "enlightened ones"), who would "over-see' the rest of humanity (in other words, control everyone else in a dictatorial world government); and, of course, the Illuminati themselves.

In 1773, when Amschel had accumulated sufficient funds through his fractional reserve and usury banking practices, he called a secret meeting in his old goldsmith shop with 12 of the most powerful and influential men of the time. 'Me purpose of this meeting was to convince the attendees to pool their resources and, with the help of his plan, gain total control of the resources of the world!

The plan Amschel laid out consisted of several steps, including:

1) Law is force in disguise. Right lies in force ("Might makes Right")... The right to rule lies in force.

2) Political freedom is an idea, not a fact. In order to usurp political power, all that is necessary is to preach 'liberalism,' and the electorates will give up more and more power to the conspirators.

3) Money is all-powerful. Governments are insignificant compared to money. Since governments control the money, that control must be removed from governments, and put in the hands of the conspirators.

4) Any and all means to achieve the goal of world domination by the conspirators is justified.

5) The size, scope, and power of the conspirators' resources must remain hidden.

6) Alcohol, drugs, and moral corruption shall be used to weaken the will of the people.

7) Wars should be instigated and orchestrated so that both sides would be in their debt (in other words, the conspirators would gain profit and power, no matter who "won" the wars!).

8) Propaganda and control of information should be used to influence opinion.

9) Pre-planned and artificially manipulated financial panics and depression should be used to tame the people, and weaken governments, so as to ultimately form a one-world government, with the conspirators as the rulers.

Amschel had 5 sons, 4 of whom he sent to the major cities of four different major powers of Europe, to establish or gain control over the major central bank of each country. Solomon went to Vienna, Austria; Nathan to London, England; Carl to Naples, Italy; James to Paris, France; while Meyer (and Amschel) stayed in Frankfurt, Germany. In addition to these major countries of Germany, Austria, England, Italy and France, the Rothschilds did extensive banking for the governments of Belgium, Spain, Brazil, and many other countries. This was all part of Amschel's plan to gain control over vast wealth and power.

By having each of his sons running successful central banks in each country, Amschel could influence the economy and politics of Europe, to create economic panics and wars... just as he had planned. Each country's banks (controlled by the Rothschilds) would then finance the wars for the conflicting countries and, as a result, the bankers would profit. If you study history, you will see that, during this period of time, there was perpetual war in Europe for many years, particularly after the Rothschilds came to power!

In essence, nearly all the wars in Europe at this time (and since) have not been fought over political ideology (which was/is merely a disguise), but to increase the wealth and power of the international banking conspiracy, through the Rothschild banking dynasty, and based on the principles of the Illuminati.

G. Edward Griffin, in 77ie Creature From *Jekyll Island* (about the history of the illegal, behind-the-scenes, establishment of the Federal Reserve), calls this purposeful pitting of one country against another, the "Rothschild Formula." He summarizes this formula as follows:

1) War is the ultimate discipline to any government. Survival from war becomes primary - everything else is secondary.

2) All that is necessary to insure government indebtedness (to the international banking conspiracy) is war - or the threat of war.

3) To create such a situation, it is necessary to pit two countries (or segments of one country) of equal force against one another - or to create them (the two opposing countries or segments of one country) if they do not already exist. ("Pit one side against the other, and finance *both* sides - so that the bankers win, no matter which side actually "wins.").

4) The ultimate obstacle to this formula is a country that is not willing to finance war through debt. When this occurs, it becomes necessary to encourage internal political conflict and/or infiltrate the government.

5) No one nation can be permitted to gain military dominance, because this would lead to a lack of conflict for power, and may lead to peace!

Peace was (and still is) unthinkable to the bankers, who profited from government war debt. This "war at all costs" formula has been played out time and time again, not only in recent years with the continuous wars in Eastern Europe since the so-called breakup of the Communist Regime (another Big Lie, which will be covered later in this report), but also through all of American history, including: the Revolution, the War of 1812, the Civil War, World War 1, World War II, the Korean War, the war in Vietnam, "Desert Storm," and practically all other conflicts - both great and small in between and since (such as Somalia, Haiti, Bosnia, etc.)! Understanding this "war at all costs" (for ultimate profit and control by the bankers) is an important insight into history.

The American Revolution

The plan of the Illuminati was extremely successful... but there suddenly appeared on the horizon a major stumbling block to the attainment of their ultimate goal of world domination which they never anticipated, and which threw them into a general panic: the newly established "government 'of the people, by the people, and for the people"... the United States of America. This was-the first-time art the history of the world that the people had actually been put into a position of power superior to their own government! The conspirators feared (and correctly so) that they would never be able to gain control over the new country if the people themselves had such previously unheard of power.

Politicians are easily corrupted with bribery, to do, think, and say whatever they are told. But to bribe an entire population would have been impossible - especially since it was the property of the people that the conspirators were after! ... Just imagine if you caught a burglar red-handed stealing your valuables. Do you think you would agree to go along with the burglar if he promised to share his loot (which he stole from you to begin with)? I don't think so! ... Obviously, the conspirators recognized immediately that the United States of America would have to be destroyed - one-way or another - if their plan of world domination were to succeed!

Ironically enough, this new government, which they viewed as their number one enemy (even in its infancy!), might never have come to power, had it not been for their infiltration and meddling in the "natural order of things." The truth is that the Revolutionary War may not have been fought, had it not been for the interference of the Bank of England (under the control of Nathan Rothschild himself) True, King George III had wronged the colonies in many ways, but not many know that King George II banned the money the colonials had been printing, at the request of the Bank of England (i.e. Nathan Rothschild), to force the colonies to use English money - which was already debt-money, based on absolutely nothing - exactly like today's "Federal Reserve Notes!"

After the American Revolution, the conspirators (specifically the Rothschilds) set to work immediately to gain control of the money of the new republic, by trying to establish a central bank (which they, of course, would control) to issue "debt money", which the people would have to borrow from them, then pay back with interest. To help them establish their central bank, they enlisted the aid of Alexander Hamilton, who had been handsomely paid to act on their behalf. They also gave him large sums of money to bribe members of Congress to vote in their favor.

Thomas Jefferson, a man of great insight and one of the finest thinkers in American history, was one of the few who understood the power of central banking. He vehemently opposed the establishment of a monopolistic central bank, and issued this warning in 1791: "If the American people ever allow the banks to control issuance of their currency, first by inflation and then by deflation, the banks will deprive the people of all property until their children wake up homeless on the continent their forefathers conquered."

Unfortunately, the bankers won (due largely to the bribes Hamilton paid Congress to vote in the bankers' favor), and the first Bank of the United States was founded in 1791. This was the beginning of a long and bloody battle for the control of the money of the American people. Who was the power behind the Bank of the United States (Important: it was not called "the Bank of the United States of America)?? Who else but the Illuminati, who were gradually developing into an international banking conspiracy, spearheaded by the Rothschilds.

By 1798 the power and influence of the Illuminati had spread far beyond their European origins. In that year, a well traveled and well-informed scholar named John Robison, and a devoutly religious cleric, the Abbey Baruelle, both wrote books to warm the world - and especially its governments, of the international power and permeation which the Illuminati already had so cunningly and so secretly achieved... thanks largely to the considerable wealth and power wielded by the Rothschilds and their growing dynasty.

Even in far away America, that infiltration into positions of influence had become a whispered scandal. So much so, in fact, that in October of 1798, George Washington, in a letter to a friend, expressed his concern over the spread in the United States of "the diabolical tenets of the Illuminati."

The secrecy of the conspiracy was gradually becoming tighter. And, although their presence could always be felt behind the scenes, the history of the Illuminati/Rothschild conspiracy itself became more and more shadowy - eventually consolidating into one organization, which blended almost imperceptibly into the background...

From 1798 until 1815, the insiders of the conspiracy were establishing themselves in positions of power within both American and European governments and institutions on both sides of the battle lines that had been drawn by Napoleon. Since it was their primary purpose to destroy all governments, and replace them with a one-world tyranny run by them, they chose to infiltrate and destroy both sides from within. (They maintain this policy even today, by manipulating both sides of any conflict, so that they come out the only winners.)

THE END OF THE BEGINNING

Meanwhile, the charter for the Bank of the United States, being for only 20 years, expired in 1811. At that it time, a great deal of economic chaos "just happened" to engulf America. In actual fact, the Rothschilds, through tremendous fluctuations in America's money supply, had created it. This was achieved largely through Nathan Rothschild, who controlled the Bank of England... which bought controlling interest in the textile manufacturing plants of the northern States, while at the same time purchasing huge supplies of cotton from the southern States. It was then a relatively simple matter to manipulate both the textile industry (by withholding the raw material, cotton), and the cotton industry (by withholding cotton to drive the price up, then dumping huge amounts on the market, to drive the price down)... a standard tactic the Rothschilds have used ever since to manipulate and control whatever market (including the Stock Market) which best suits their interests...

This manipulation caused wild fluctuations in the prices of both cotton and textiles (and thus profits and wages), severely affecting the money supply available to the public, which the small, private bankers could not keep up with. As a result of this behind-the-scenes manipulation, which the conspirators falsely attributed to the "normal behavior of the fickle marketplace," the public clamored for "more stability" in the banking industry. Thus, Nathan Rothschild upheld Amschel's (and the Illuminati's) plan: to create reasons (problems) to justify creating a second central bank, so the banking cartel could maintain control.

But it didn't work... or at least, it was not enough. The bankers needed a war (their favorite tool), to bring about the creation of the second Bank of the United States. But as no war was imminent, they did what they had already done before, and what they have also done on countless occasions since. They *created* one! Hence, the War of 1812!

The war of 1812 was one of the most senseless wars in history (unless you know the bankers' plot!) It was supposed fought over impressments of American sailors into the British navy, to serve in fighting the French. It is strange that America did not also go to war with the French, who had been doing the same thing for years... especially since the practice of impressments by the British had ceased *before* the war!

The monetary cost of fighting a war created by the bankers, in addition to the economic trauma of inflation and large boom-bust cycles (caused by so-called "private banking, even though it was still highly regulated, government controlled, and monopolized by the banking conspiracy - just without a central bank) gave significant impetus to form the second Bank of the United States.

This second bank was almost identical to the first bank, and in no way did it put an end to the boom-bust cycles. In fact, it made them worse. In reality, the boom-bust cycles (today called inflation and recession) were created because there was a lack of real free enterprise banking with unsubsidized free competition. The ensuing years saw great economic hardship culminating in the panic of 1819.

These artificially created boom-bust cycles continued for several years until Andrew Jackson became president in 1828. Jackson was a staunch opponent to the central bank, and recognized that the second Bank of the U.S. had already done a great deal of damage to America and her economy. He also realized that the Bank of the U.S. was merely a tool used by the international Rothschild/Illuminati conspiracy to gain complete control over the fledgling nation and destroy it from within. In a valiant attempt to preserve the ideals of freedom and individual sovereignty on which America was founded, he swore to free the country from the bankers' evil, greedy grasp.

He wrote:

"Is there no danger to our liberty and independence in a bank that in its nature has so little to bind it to our country? ... [Is there not] cause to tremble for the purity of our elections in peace and for the independence of our country in war? ... [There can be no doubt that] the course which would be pursued by a bank almost wholly owned by the subjects of a foreign power, and managed by those interests, would run in the same direction... Controlling our currency, receiving our public monies, and holding thousands of our citizens in dependence, it would be more formidable and dangerous than a naval and military power of the enemy!"

In this statement, Jackson reveals that the Second Bank of the United States was controlled by a foreign power and that it was a threat to the sovereignty of the U.S. This is a significant piece of evidence supporting a conspiracy at that time. Ultimately, the issue of the central bank became so volatile that Jackson based his entire re-election campaign on the bank. His campaign slogan was: "Jackson and no bank, or bank and no Jackson."

Unfortunately, the head of the bank at that time, Nicholas Biddle, had gained control over most of the Congress by lining the pockets of the Congressmen! Congressman John Randolph from Virginia noted the corruption: "Every man you meet in this House [of Representatives] or out of it, with some rare exceptions, which only serve to prove the rule, is either a stockholder, president, cashier, clerk, or doorkeeper, runner, engraver, paper-maker, or mechanic in some other way to the Bank!"

As a result of Jackson's views (and the fact that so much of Congress had been bribed or "bought off"), Jackson was censured by the Senate. An attempt on Jackson's life was also made in 1835, but both of the would-be assassin's pistols misfired, leaving Jackson unharmed! The assassin, Richard Lawrence, was later found not guilty on grounds of insanity. Lawrence later claimed that he had been "in touch with the powers of Europe," which promised to intervene if any attempt was made to punish him.

In 1836, soon after the attempt on his life, Jackson said to the bankers, "You are a den of vipers. I intend to rout you out, and by the Eternal God, I will rout you out! If the people only understood the rank injustice of our money and banking system, there would be a revolution before morning!"

Ultimately, Jackson won, and the charter for the second Bank of the United States expired without renewal in 1836. This victory was not without its price, however. Biddle, the head of the bank, in a last ditch grab for power, drastically curtailed the money supply, causing severe deflation. This was made even worse by the Bank of England, as historian Henry Clews explains: "The Panic of 1837 was aggravated by the Bank of England when it - in one day - called in all the paper [currency] connected with the United States."

As a result, there was continuing economic disruption right up until the Civil War. This was due largely to interference by the international banking cartel, headed by the Rothschilds, who continued to create boom-bust cycles through their vast monetary influence... By now, you should begin to understand that the international banking cartel would (and still will) do anything to gain power.

In fact, by 1848 the conspiracy was cohesive enough, powerful enough, and with sufficient reach, to have brought on the various revolutions and uprisings of that year almost simultaneously in several countries!

At the same time, a radical action-arm of the conspiracy, know as the communist movement, came out more or less openly on the scene, with an announcement of its existence, its methods, and its purposes. This was done through the publication in 1848 of "The Communist Manifesto," through a group of conspirators known as "the League of Just Men."

They commissioned a young intellectual named Karl Marx to prepare a summary of the strategy, tactics, principles, and aims of the newly emerging "communist movement." Marx prepared this summary with the help of a wealthy fellow revolutionary and close friend, Frederick Engles. Contrary to the impression that has been so carefully created since, there was almost nothing original on the part of Marx and Engles in "The Communist Manifesto"... In fact, their names did not even appear on any copy of the manifesto when it first came neither out, nor for at least 20 years thereafter! In reality, the Communist Manifesto was simply a thinly disguised version of "the Rothschild plan" of achieving world domination! It - along with the numerous revolutions and insurrections of 1848 - marked the beginning of a new era in the history of the conspiracy... that of the overt manipulation of governments, and the orchestration of events - both of which were to serve the conspiracy's goals of world domination.

The Civil War

"If destruction be our lot, we must ourselves be its author and finisher. As a nation of freemen, we must live through all times, or die by suicide " - Abraham Lincoln

There is a common belief (promoted by the conspiracy-owned media, and the conspiracy-owned major publishing houses as we *will* discuss in another section) that the Civil War was fought over slavery. It is true that slavery played a role in the *Civil* War, but the false presumption that slavery *caused* the war is just another example of the international conspirators using "the plight of the down-trodden masses" to achieve their goals - just as they did with the establishment of the Communist Regime (also covered later in this report)! ... The actual truth is that the Civil War "broke out" after much meticulous planning and subterfuge, to achieve the conspirators' goal of re-establishing a central bank in the United States! Numerous previous attempts, using bribery and coercion of Congress, had failed. This left the conspirators no choice but to resort to the tried-and-true Illuminati/Rothschild doctrine of "pitting one side against the other."

'Me international banking conspiracy essentially manipulated the conflicting economic interests of the North and the South, which undoubtedly could have been resolved by negotiation, until they achieved a full-blown war... funding both sides and reaping the resulting financial harvest from both sides - just as they had always done, and still do to this day!

The actual reason that the war broke out had absolutely nothing to do with slavery! In fact, Lincoln himself pointed out the conflict in economic interests of both sides, and in his campaign for the presidency, stated that *he would not interfere in the practice of slavery.* He even repeated this message in his first inaugural address:

"Apprehension seems to exist among the people of the Southern States, that, by the accession of a Republican administration, their peace and personal security are to be endangered... I have no purpose, directly or indirectly, to interfere with the institution of slavery in the states where it now exists. I believe I have no lawful right to do so, and I have no inclination to do so!"

Even after the outbreak of the war in 1861, Lincoln confirmed his previous stand. He said: "My paramount object in this struggle is to save the Union, and it is *not* either to save or destroy slavery. If I could save the Union without freeing any slave, I would do it, and if I could save it by freeing all of the slaves, I would do it, and if I could save it by freeing some and leaving others alone, I would also do that."

It is clear that Lincoln was not a crusader against slavery. He was merely trying to hold together the Union. But if it was not slavery that was tearing the Union apart, what was it? The answer comes partly from the economic conflict between the North and South, and also once again from the international banking conspiracy.

Economic conflict arose because the South was trading much of its cotton with England for manufactured goods, as opposed to trading with the North. (Remember how the Bank of England, controlled by Nathan Rothschild, had already acquired controlling interests in textile manufacturing plants in the North, while at the same time purchased huge quantities of cotton from the South?) To force more trade between the north and south as opposed to foreign (especially English) powers, the U.S. government imposed heavy tariffs on English imports. This forced the southern states to pay more for all of their imported goods, while at the same time causing other countries to which the South exported cotton, to enact tariffs of their own.

But the greatest amount of tension between the States was directly created by the international banking cartel, headed by the Rothschild family. Since the defeat of the second Bank of the U.S., the bankers, both through Congress and by causing harmful boom-bust cycles, had been attempting to establish a new centralized bank, but without success. They had to try another strategy. An even greater incentive was needed to force the U.S. into creating another central bank this was where the Civil War and the use of the Rothschild Formula came in. As noted earlier, *the "Rothschild Formula. Consists of pitting one country (or section of a country) against another, to allow the bankers to gain power and enormous profit!* The international banking cartel wanted to use this formula against the U.S., but could find no realistic adversary. Canada and Mexico were far too inferior in-economic and military strength to challenge the U.S., and the European powers were too far away to wage an effective war on American soil. So, in the true Rothschild fashion, they decided to create a conflict, using the issue of slavery to divide the North and South. This division was explained by the Chancellor of Germany at that time, Otto von Bismarck:

"The division of the United States into two federations of equal force was decided long before the Civil War, by the high financial powers of Europe. These bankers were afraid that the United States, if they remained in one block and as one nation, would attain economic and financial independence, which would upset their financial domination over the world! The voice of the Rothschilds prevailed. They saw tremendous booty if they could substitute two feeble democracies, burdened with debt to the financiers, in place of the vigorous Republic, sufficient unto herself. Therefore, they sent their emissaries into the field to exploit the question of slavery and to open an abyss between the two sections of the Union."

Once the war had broken out, it was made even more volatile, as the French government (influenced by James Rothschild) landed troops in Mexico, and the British government (influenced by Nathan Rothschild) landed troops in Canada - both of which would have sided with the South. This was done mainly because the South was even more outmatched than popular (i.e. conspiracy approved) history acknowledges. In response to this, President Lincoln asked for and received assistance from the Russian Czar, Alexander.

Alexander's motive for helping the U.S. was twofold. First, he had recently freed all the surfs in his country, and thought what the North was doing was just. But more importantly, he also felt the threat and power of the international banking conspirators (who were also attempting to break up Russia), and understood that their defeat would be in his own best interests. The Russian navy was sent out to help set up a blockade of the South. The most significant effect of this, however, was that it kept both the French and the English out of the war. Neither of them wanted a war with both the *U.S. and* Russia.

Although Russia's assistance helped a great deal, most of the people of the North correctly thought of the war as a war for the business interests (not slavery). So how could they be induced to fight? The problem was solved when Lincoln issued the Emancipation Proclamation, which effectively turned the war into an anti-slavery crusade, and which was also used as a friendly gesture toward the Czar of Russia.

As the Civil War progressed, the North really began feeling the economic squeeze caused by the international banking cartel, which had drastically reduced the North's money supply. Then, when the bankers felt the timing was right, they moved in for the kill... They approached Lincoln with loan offers at 27% interest! He turned them down flat... Lincoln was no man's fool. He saw right through the banking cartel's insulting offer of "help", recognizing it immediately for what it actually was: a thinly veiled attempt to get back in total control of America's money.

Right after he was approached with the bankers'

outrageous offer, Lincoln solved the North's money crunch by authorizing the printing of "Green Backs", which was un-backed paper currency. He realized, since the money the banking cartel offered him was based on nothing (non gold backed), that he could print and use money based on nothing just as well as they could, without paying ridiculous interest rates on it! 'Me bankers were furious about Lincoln's presumptuous act! They felt that he was usurping "their" power. Even worse, they were afraid that leaders in other countries might follow Lincoln's lead and start printing their own money also, which would mean the end of their power grabbing and thus the end of their plan to rule the world. Lincoln had to be stopped! Sensing his imminent danger, Lincoln said: "I have two great enemies, the Southern Army in front of me, and the financial institutions in the rear. Of the two, the one in the rear is the greatest enemy."

By heavily bribing and threatening congressional Representatives and Senators through their numerous insider spies and agents, the banking cartel managed to get the National Banking Act rammed through Congress, and passed on February 25th, 1863. This Act established a new system of nationally chartered banks similar to the Bank of the United States, but used money that was not backed by gold.

Lincoln vehemently opposed the Act, saying: "The money power preys upon the nation in times of peace and conspires against it in times of adversity. It is more despotic than monarchy, more insolent than autocracy, more selfish than bureaucracy. I see in the near future a crisis approaching that unnerves me and causes me to tremble for the safety of my country. Corporations have been enthroned, an era of corruption will follow, and the money power of the country will endeavor to prolong its reign by working upon the prejudices of the people, until all the wealth is aggregated in a few hands, and the Republic destroyed!"

The National Banking Act was strongly supported, however by Secretary of the Treasury, Salomon P. Chase, later of Chase Manhattan, one of the banking cartel banks (What a surprise! ... By the way, Chase Manhattan is one of the owners of today's Federal Reserve, and controlled by none other than David Rockefeller, a staunch proponent of the impending world dictatorship). With this Act, the banking cartel had nearly succeeded in instituting another national bank, and began their plunder of America all over again by collecting heavy interest from the government war debt. Still, it was not enough. The system was similar to our present day Federal Reserve, but it couldn't do everything the banking conspirators wanted - it couldn't do everything the Federal Reserve does.

Ultimately, the North won the war and the Union held, at an astronomical cost to the U.S. in lives and money. The bankers were the real winners, however, reaping enormous profits while managing at the same time to install the foundation of a totalitarian banking monopoly system! Even in victory, they did not forget what they rightly considered to be their greatest threat to developing and profiting from this new, powerful tool (a totalitarian banking monopoly) a knowledgeable and stalwart President, who would not be intimidated or bribed, and who had established un-backed money ("Green Backs") without the aid of the bankers. Just as an attempt was made on President Jackson's life because he was against the bankers, so was one made on Lincoln's life.... This time they were successful... (There is substantial evidence connecting John Wilkes Booth to both the Illuminati and the Rothschilds.)

Our history books (published by conspiracy owned or controlled publishing houses) teach us that the outcome of the Civil war was positive for 2 reasons: 1) the United States stayed united; and 2) slavery was finally abolished... But as far as the international banking conspiracy was concerned, the outcome of the Civil War was positive for a very different reason: It provided the conspirators with the opportunity to take advantage of the one major flaw - the single error - of our founding fathers. That flaw was in granting the federal government dictatorial powers over its own jurisdiction, the District of Columbia.

In 1965, the 13th Amendment abolished slavery and involuntary servitude except as punishment for a crime. The 13th Amendment did allow for "voluntary servitude," but did nothing to specifically define this condition. This was just the "chink in the armor" that the international banking conspiracy needed to destroy, once and for all, the sovereignty of the individual American citizens (which under the Constitution, guaranteed them superiority over the government). The conspirators immediately recognized that all they needed to do was to trick the American people into "voluntarily" giving up their sovereignty! ... But how?

'Me 13th Amendment freed the slaves, but it did not make them citizens, much less sovereigns - thus they had no protection under the law. To rectify this situation, the 14th Amendment was added in 1868, which made the freed slaves citizens. But under the Constitution, the Federal government did not have the power or jurisdiction to make the freed slaves sovereign State citizens - only birth to sovereign parents could do that. But the Constitution did grant the Federal government unlimited (or absolute dictatorial) powers within its jurisdiction, so the only solution seemed to be that of allowing the newly freed slaves the status of "citizens" under the Federal jurisdiction, which is exactly what they did. As a result, the 14th Amendment created, for the first time in American history, a "citizen of the United States" (in other words, a "citizen of - or under the jurisdiction of - the United States Federal government"). This new class of "citizen" was created by the Federal government, and therefore "subject to" the Federal government -its creator... as opposed to the Constitutional Sovereign citizen, who is the creator of - and therefore superior to - the government.

The 14th Amendment also made the freed slave a citizen (or "resident") of the state in which he resided... Now - just as in a dictatorship or monarchy - the Federal government had its own "subjects"... And the States themselves had two classes of "citizens": 1) the sovereign citizen, who was superior to all governments - local, state, and federal; and 2) the resident citizen, who was subject (inferior) to all governments - federal, state and local.

The machinery was in place. Now all the international banking conspiracy had to do was trick the sovereign citizens into voluntary servitude to the federal- government by admitting to being citizens of (and therefore subject - or inferior to) the Federal government. They eventually did this through the Federal Reserve, and numerous socialist programs (as we will soon see). There was still some initial groundwork to be laid, however, so they immediately set to work on it...

THE BEGINNING OF THE END

The next 45 years saw little major upheaval from the banking conspiracy. They still kept up their usual antics of market manipulation for profit, as well as applying gradualism to gain more power - most noticeably in the Federal government just as Amschel Rothschild's plan called, for. The conspirators were seemingly satisfied for the time being... Unfortunately, they had regained their foothold in American banking, which would later allow them to totally dominate the American economy (as they do today).

During these 45 years, the international banking conspiracy was actually laying careful groundwork to implement what would be their most brilliant and diabolical instrument for dealing the final death-blow to what they considered their greatest enemy in the establishment of their totalitarian one-world government: The United States of America, with its sovereign citizens in superiority over America's "government of the people, by the people, and for the people."

America has never recovered from the next step which they unscrupulously and meticulously devised. In fact, the United States of America is today in its final death throws, and unless enough citizens are made aware of the horrible crimes of treachery, fraud, theft and even murder that the evil and unscrupulous international banking cartel (with the help of selfish, greedy and self-serving politicians) has perpetrated against our country, our liberty, our property, and our very lives, then our "America the Beautiful, Sweet Land of Liberty" will cease to exist - probably within the next 5 years or less (their target date for establishing the "New World Order" has been set at the year 2000 to the year 2002 and our children will grow up as slaves (no more than mere "biological units", or chattel) to the most ruthless and horrifying dictatorship we have ever seen!

Let's examine this terrifying yet brilliant "instrument of death" which has already (over 60 years ago!) struck its fatal blow to our once great Republic! ...

The Federal Reserve

"Permit me to control the currency of a nation, and I care not who makes its laws!" - Amschel Rothschild

Since Colonial times - even before the American Revolution, there have been scores of financial atrocities committed against the people of the United States, but all pale in comparison to the creation of the Federal Reserve! From day one this unspeakable monstrosity has put enormous power over the entire population directly into the hands of a few elite through the international banking conspiracy (who also control the rest of the world), through complete control of the nation's wealth, resources, and (of course!) money... Now, unfortunately, we at last understand the prophetic statement: "the love of money is the root of all evil." The international banking cartel (and their well-paid servants in the form of politicians, and members of the judicial, legal and so-called law-enforcement agencies), in their relentless and nearly completed quest for total control over the entire planet, and everything that is good, honest, decent and moral, for their ultimate goal of total world domination!

The story of the Federal Reserve begins in a train station in Hoboken, New Jersey, where 5 bankers, a Senator, and the US Assistant Secretary of the Treasury secretly boarded a train destined for Jekyll Island, Georgia, on November 22nd, 1910. The five bankers were: Frank A Vanderlipp, president of National City Bank of New York (representing the interests of the Rockefellers, and of the banking house of Kuhn, Loeb & Company); Henry P. Davis, senior partner of the J.P. Morgan Company; Charles D. Norton, president of J.P. Morgan's First National Bank of New York; Benjamin Strong, head of J.P. Morgan's Bankers Trust Company; and Paul M. Warburg, a Rothschild agent who was salaried at $500,000 a year (more than $5 million today), and a partner in Kuhn, Loeb & Company. 'Me Senator was Nelson W. Aldrich, maternal grandfather of Nelson Aldrich Rockefeller. The Assistant Secretary of the Treasury was Abraham Piatt Andrew.

The meeting was kept very secret because, as with all conspiracies, discovery would mean defeat. J.P. Morgan, the notorious banker and industrialist (not -to mention agent of the Rothschilds), often took guests to this hunting club, so it did not *seem* out of the ordinary. But in fact, this meeting marked the beginning of the most extraordinary, brilliant, cunning, and unabashedly *evil* step toward their ultimate goal of world domination that the international banking conspiracy had ever attempted!

The purpose of this week-long meeting was to design a central bank, based on the National Banking Act of 1863, that would give the international banking conspirators even more power, and allow them to reap even greater profits through the U.S. government.

Senator Aldrich was present to make sure that the bill would pass Congress. Paul Warburg, the most knowledgeable banker, was the main architect of the plan. The other bankers were there to help work out the details of the plan, and to make sure that their superiors' interests were represented... James Warburg, son of Paul Warburg, later made clear what the banking conspiracy's goal was (and still is to this day): "We shall have world government whether you like it or not - if not by consent, by conquest!"

You may ask, "Why would a group of *private bankers* who already had a monopoly on the banking system, create the Federal Reserve?" The answer lies in the fact that they had been working toward something like this for some time, and as a result they had achieved increasing wealth, power and control over both the government and the media, allowing them to do a slick job of marketing the plan to both Congress and the public.

Until the creation of the Federal Reserve, there had been an on-going struggle in the U.S. for control of the nation's money. The international banking cartel, headed by the Rothschilds and fronted in the U.S. by J.P. Morgan and others, had gradually gained greater and greater control of American banking, primarily by monopolizing the commercial banks, influencing interest rates, and by causing massive boom/bust cycles in the economy. They had money and they had power ... but it wasn't enough. They wanted *all* the money and *total* power. The Federal Reserve was the key factor that would give them *complete control of the U.S. monetary system.*

The few years preceding the creation of this plan saw increasing social and economic turbulence, culminating with the Panic of 1907. In the fall of that year, J.P. Morgan's interests manipulated the financial industry to artificially create the Panic, killing off rival banks or consolidating them within the Morgan financial monopoly. This was all part of the Rothschild plan, as historian Ralph Epperson, author of *7he Unseen Hand* (an excellent book about the conspiracy) explains:

"So the American people, who had suffered through the American Revolution, the War of 1812, the battles between Andrew Jackson and the Second Bank of the United States, the Civil War, the previous panics of 1873 and 1898, and now the Panic of 1907, were finally conditioned to the point of accepting the solution offered by those who had caused all of theses events: the international bankers!"

One amazing aspect of this story is how the bankers made sure that they would have a president in the White House that they could be certain would sign the bill (the Federal Reserve Act). The election of 1912 would obviously decide which president would face the bill. Republican Robert Taft was up for re-election, and was on the record as saying that he would veto the bill! To counter this, the bankers fully backed Democrat Woodrow Wilson, who had already promised them he would sign the bill into law! The only problem was, Taft had a strong lead in the polls. So, to insure Wilson's victory, the bankers also convinced ex-President Theodore Roosevelt to run in the election, under the flag of the "Bull Moose Party." The bankers funded Roosevelt's campaign in the hopes of diverting enough votes from Taft to Roosevelt so as to put Wilson in the White House. The plan worked. Wilson won with 45% of the vote. Since almost all of the votes for Roosevelt came from Taft's voter base, Taft would have easily defeated Wilson had Roosevelt not run -and the Federal Reserve Act would have been vetoed...

[An almost identical situation recently occurred in the 1992 presidential election. Although George Bush was a supporter of the "New World Order," he was not in favor of completely demolishing the sovereignty of the United States. Bill Clinton, on the other hand, is a strong supporter of a one-world government into which the national identity and sovereignty of the United Stated will be completely absorbed. Enter billionaire candidate Ross Perot, who dropped out of the race supposedly when it became apparent that he didn't have enough voter base to win... but then mysteriously (on the urging of the banking cartel) re-entered the race - just in time to divert enough votes from Bush supporters to assure a Clinton victory!)

Another key to getting the Federal Reserve Act enacted was to make sure that it would pass Congress. Senator Aldrich used as much of his influence as he could muster, but it wasn't enough. Massive media and propaganda blitzes were used to convince both the public and Congress that the bill was in the best interests of the people. But still more was needed...

So the conspirators devised an ingenious plan of introducing the bill in two formats at two different times. The first time, it was introduced in Congress as the "Aldrich Plan." Senator Aldrich, a Republican, was a known supporter of "big business," which is really just another name for the international banking conspiracy (since they had already systematically gained controlling interests in almost all large international businesses and corporations). So the "Aldrich Plan" was purposely touted by the big bankers, and at the same time bombarded with negative publicity by the banking cartel's propaganda machine known as the "media". This may seem counterproductive, but in reality, they were *trying* to get the bill shot down, so it would look like the "banker bill" was no more. An almost identical bill was then "drawn up" and submitted a few weeks later by two Democrats: Senator Robert Owen and Congressman Carter Glass. This was first known as the Glass-Owen bill, and later as the "Federal Reserve Act." In a superb act of deceit, the bankers criticized the bill to make it appear as though it was not what they wanted! Frank Vanderlipp, who was part of the original, clandestine meeting on Jekyll Island, later revealed to *The Saturday Evening Post:* "Although the Aldrich Federal Reserve Plan was defeated when it bore the name 'Aldrich,' its essential points were all contained in the plan that finally was adopted. "

Through these subversive tactics, the bankers got general acceptance of the Federal Reserve Act. Some compromises were necessary, however, before Congress could pass it in its final form. It was already just a few days before Christmas, and Congress was told that the act would not be ready to be voted on until after the holiday recess. In one last act of treachery, the bill came up again for a final vote on December 22nd, 1913. Most congressmen had already gone home for the holidays. Those few left (there was not even a quorum present!) were taken by surprise, and unprepared to vote on it, not having even been given the chance to read the "final" version thoroughly. Thus, they cast their votes based solely on what the popular opinion expressed in the "media" was...

An example of the propaganda at that time comes from an article entitled "A Better System of Banking and Currency," in *The Independent,* a paper owned by Nelson Aldrich: "[The Federal Reserve] is an ideal method of fighting a monopoly. It could not possibly itself become a monopoly, and it would prevent other banks from combining into monopolies. With earnings limited to four and one-half percent [emphasis added], there could not be a monopoly."

On that very day - December 22nd, 1913 - just one day before President Woodrow Wilson signed the Federal Reserve Act into law, Congressman Charles Lindbergh, Sr. (father of the famous aviator) said:

"'Me money trust deliberately caused the 1907 panic, and thereby forced Congress to create a National Monetary Commission, which led to the ultimate creation of the Federal Reserve. This Federal Reserve Act establishes the most gigantic monetary trust [monopoly] on earth. When the President signs this bill, the invisible government of the monetary power will be legalized. 'Me people may not know it immediately, but the day of reckoning is only a few years removed... The people must make a declaration of independence to relieve them from the monetary power. This they will be able to do by taking control of Congress. Wall Streeters; could not cheat us if you Senators and Representatives did not make a humbug of Congress... The greatest crime against Congress is its currency system. This banking bill perpetrates the worst legislative crime of the ages. The caucus and party bosses have again operated and prevented the people from getting the benefits of their own government."

Lindbergh also made this observation: "Ever since the Civil War, Congress has allowed the bankers to completely control financial legislation. The membership of the

Finance Committee in the Senate and the Committee on Banking and Currency in the House has been made up of bankers, their agents and attorneys. These committees have controlled the nature of the bills to be reported, the extent of them, and the debates that were to be held on them when they were being considered in the Senate and the House. No one who is not on the committees is recognized, unless someone favorable to the committees [the banking interests] has been arranged for.

Congressman Wright Patman, the Chairman of the House Banking and Currency Committee agreed with Lindbergh when he said, "In the United States today, we have in effect two governments. We have the duly constituted government. Then we have an independent, uncontrolled and un-coordinated [that is, not coordinated with the formal, "constitutional" government] government in the Federal Reserve System, illegally operating the money powers which are reserved to Congress by the Constitution."

Yet, the damage had been done. The international banking cartel had their dream of a centralized monopoly bank of the U.S. The powers granted to the bankers under the Federal Reserve Act were everything they wanted. Although the American public as a whole did not know that their country had been taken over, nor the danger and destruction this control would mean. The bankers were counting on the ignorance of Americans, and worked very hard (with the help of the "media", which they already controlled) to maintain that ignorance. Furthermore, the bankers were prepared to permanently silence anyone who threatened exposure of their scheme (Remember: Exposure = Defeat).

"But what can be so bad about creating a central banking system?" you might ask. Because with so much power, the bankers suddenly had the ability to legally steal the American people blind... That was the banking conspiracy's sole purpose in creating the Federal Reserve in the first place... and that is exactly what they have done. Let's find out how...

Essentially, the Federal Reserve creates money by entering into the records that a certain amount of money was created. Then they order the U.S. Treasury to have the money printed. This money is not backed by anything (like gold or silver). It is merely *paper and ink.* The Federal Reserve then pays the U.S. Mint for the paper, ink, and the printing of the money. This comes to approximately two and one-half cents per bill (no matter what the denomination. $1 ... $500... $10,000... it doesn't matter. It still costs the Federal Reserve only $.025 for every bill!). Then The Federal Reserve turns around and "lends" the money to the United States government - at full face *value... plus interest!* The government (or actually the American citizenry) is then in "debt" to the Federal Reserve, and is obligated to payback the full amount supposedly "borrowed", plus *the interest!*

Anytime anyone borrows money, new money is "created." So in effect, the Federal Reserve makes a profit, not only on the interest paid on the money that they simply printed out of nothing, but they also make a profit by demanding that the original amount of the so-called "loan", also be paid back *in full to* phrase that another way, the Federal Reserve (and therefore the international banking conspiracy which *owns* the Federal Reserve) simply orders money to be printed, then "lends" that "money" out to our government, and demands that our government "repay" the "money" lent, plus interest on the so-called "money"!! In case you still don't understand, they never had any money to start with, to loan out! All they did was pay (a very modest fee) to have the money printed!

Imagine, if you will: You decide to lend money to the government, so all you do is take some "camera-ready-copies of whatever you decide are "legal tender" to your local Office Depot or other copy shop. You pay the copy shop for printing the "paper" (because that's all it is!), and then you "lend" this very same "paper" to the government. Then you demand that the government pay you back the entire amount of whatever you supposedly "lent" to the government (depending on what you told Office Depot to print on the "bills"), plus *interest, in whatever amount you decide at the time of the transaction!!*

"Ridiculous!" you say? Well, that's exactly what the international banking conspiracy has done to our country (through the Federal Reserve, with the help of our corrupted government), since the Federal Reserve Act was illegally and fraudulently imposed on the United States of America in 1913!

If you don't believe me, listen to what Peter T. Whitte, a *National Geographic* writer, discovered when he interviewed a spokesperson for the Federal Reserve regarding where our "money" comes from:

"'We created it,' a Fed official tells me. He means that anytime the central bank writes a check, so to speak, it creates money. 'It's money that didn't exist before,' he says.

"'Is there any limit to that?' I asked. "No limit, only the good judgment and the conscience of the responsible Federal Reserve people.' ("Good judgment and conscience" from a "responsible" pack of liars, thieves, traitors, and murderers??!)

And where did they get this vast authority? "It was delegated to 'them' in the Federal Reserve Act of 1913, based on the Constitution, Article I Section 8: *'Congress-shall have the power... to coin money and regulate the value thereof...* '"

The Fed representative failed to mention that the Constitution said "coin" money, not "print" it, and that the Federal Reserve is not Congress, nor that the Federal Reserve is a private cartel of bankers. Furthermore, all US money (still popularly called "dollars", although they are actually "Federal Reserve Notes") is based on debt. The only way money is currently created is when someone - either the government or other banks, borrows money from the Fed. Every time someone borrows money from the Fed, new money is created. If all debt were ever paid off, there would be no money!! In the words of Robert Hemphill, ex-chairman of the Federal Reserve Bank of Atlanta:

"If all the bank loans were paid, no one could have a bank deposit, and there would not be a dollar of coin or currency in circulation! This is a staggering thought. We are completely dependent on the commercial banks. Someone has to borrow every dollar we have in circulation - cash or credit. If the banks create ample synthetic money, we are prosperous... if not, we starve. We are absolutely without a permanent money system. When one gets a complete grasp of the picture, the tragic absurdity of our hopeless situation is almost incredible - but there it is!"

G. Edward Griffin, author of *The Creature From Jekyll Island,* clarifies the "tragic absurdity of our hopeless situation":

"The loop through which it [money] travels can be large or small, but the fact remains that all interest is paid eventually by human effort. And the significance of that fact is even more startling than the assumption that not enough money is created to pay back the interest. It is that the total of this human effort ultimately is for the benefit of those who create fiat (un-backed) money. It is a form of modern serfdom in which the great mass of society works as indentured servants to a ruling class of financial nobility!"

If this is all beginning to sound a lot like racketeering on the scale of a full-blown dictatorship, it's because that is exactly what it is! Remember, the Federal Reserve is just one arm of the international bankers' conspiracy, which by this time in 1913, had already grown to the most powerful force the world has ever known, with unbelievable (and largely unseen) reach and influence... So who actually are these conspirators - these international racketeers - who own the Federal Reserve and in turn control its awesome power? Although the Federal Reserve Act of 1913 provided that the names of owner banks be kept a secret, R.E. McMaster, publisher of the newsletter, *The Reaper,* discovered through confidential Swiss banking connections that controlling interest in the Federal Reserve is held by ten powerful banks, owned or largely controlled by the Rothschilds. The banks are:

1) Rothschild Banks of London and Berlin

2) Lazard Brothers Bank of Paris

3) Israel Moses Sieff Bank of Italy

4) Warburg Batiks of Hamburg and Amsterdam

5) Lehman Brothers Bank of New York

6) Kuhn Loeb Bank of New York

7) Chase Manhattan Bank of New York (controlled by the Rockefellers)

8) Goldman Sachs Bank of New York

These, then, are the owners of not only the Federal Reserve, but also the entire United States of America! Given that infamous roster of ownership, it becomes clear that it is not "the people" who benefited from the creation of the Federal Reserve, but the International banking cartel!

It is important to remember that the Federal Reserve was supposedly created to put an end to the boom-bust cycles in the economy. But, of course, the exact opposite was true. The bankers used the centralized monopoly of the Fed to create even worse swings in the economy (today called "inflation" and "recession"), which they did (and *still* do) purposely, to line their own pockets, while driving America to the brink of bankruptcy... so they could one day seize complete control of the entire country! (That day is coming within the next five years or less - right on schedule with their 'target date' of the year 2000!)

The Federal Reserve has in fact *created* (under orders from their banking conspiracy owners): the Great Depression of 1929-39; the severe recessions of 1953, 1957, 1969, 1975 and 1981; the stock market crash of 1987; and the prolonged recession which has engulfed our economy ever since late 1989. They have used these so-called (artificially created and manipulated by *them)* "crises", to induce gradual inflation, which has destroyed nearly 95% of the dollar's value! ... Obviously, the Federal Reserve is the problem, not the solution!

Dr, Anthony Sutton, author of *Wall Street-and the Bolshevik Revolution,* explains what the banking cartel wanted to accomplish: "The financiers... could by government control... more easily avoid the rigors of competition. Through political influence, they could manipulate the police power of the state to achieve what they had been unable to achieve under the private enterprise system. In other words, the police power of the state was a means of maintaining a private monopoly. "

Even the House Banking Committee itself acknowledges the ultimate (and therefore unconstitutional) power of the Fed, saying that; "the Federal Reserve is, in practice, independent of that body [Congress] in its policy making... The Federal Reserve neither requires nor seeks approval of any branch of government for its policies. *The system itself decides at what ends its policies are aimed, and then takes whatever actions it sees fit to reach those ends!*

In summary, the Federal Reserve was conceived of iniquity, foisted on the American people with deceit, is a private monopoly bank that profits the few at the expense of many, does not serve its intended purpose of currency stability, is one of the planks of the *Communist Manifesto,* and is an instrument of totalitarian control. To I've with it means certain destruction of our currency, our economic system, and our national sovereignty. To live without it and other government interference in banking (as prescribed by the Constitution), means sound money and banking practices...

Some fear that undergoing such a dramatic change, as the abolition of the Fed would mean some difficult times. I would ask those people, "What do you think we are facing now? If these aren't already 'difficult times', then I don't know what is!" True, we are not currently in the midst of a severe depression, but to continue with the Federal Reserve System would mean a total collapse of our currency! This is in fact, exactly what they are planning... By the year 2,000, the international banking conspiracy intends to force the collapse of all major currencies. They have already begun this process. The United States will be called on time and again to "bail out" each country as they go under, with the bankers collecting a huge windfall on each "bail out" (this process has already begun with Mexico as the first country). Finally, the United States economy will also collapse under the unimaginable weight of the gargantuan (and totally artificially created) financial burden. Then, our friendly international bankers will step in to "save the world" from certain economic ruin and chaos - created by *them - and* propose a one-world monetary system... followed of course by a one-world court system, to maintain "integrity" in trade and commerce, and a one-world government to enforce the courts and the monetary system! ...

But we are getting ahead of ourselves. Let's continue with what Dr. Anthony Sutton referred to as using the police power of the state as a means of maintaining this private banking monopoly ("monstrosity" would be more accurate!).

The IRS and the Graduated Income Tax

"None are more hopelessly enslaved than those who falsely believe they are free!" Johann W. von Goethe

On February 25th, 1913, the Graduated Income tax was also passed, becoming the 16th Amendment to the Constitution. It is important to remember that a "graduated" income tax was one of the planks of the Communist Manifesto, and that the Constitution itself declares (and has been upheld in the Supreme Court numerous times) that any form of "income tax" could not be levied against the citizens, as the citizens were guaranteed the absolute rights to 100% of the fruits of their labors.

Furthermore, the Constitution itself states that "the United States Constitution cannot be in conflict with itself," and that any amendment, clause, law, statute, or code, which is in conflict with the Constitution, is automatically rendered *null and void!* The unscrupulous drafters of the 16th Amendment knew this, so they used fraud and deceit (and the 14th Amendment) to word the 16th Amendment in such a way that the average person could be coerced into believing that the graduated income tax was indeed Constitutional, just, right, and even "patriotic"! Time and space do not permit me to go into all the details here of how this unmitigated fraud was foisted upon an unsuspecting and trusting American public. Essentially, they used common, every day words such as "person", "citizen", "income", etc. to which they gave new, "legal" definitions (of which the average American was completely unaware) to trick the people of America into admitting that they were not "sovereign citizens" - superior to their government (as is their birthright under the laws of God, and protected by our Constitution), but that they were instead "civil citizens" (as defined by the 14th Amendment) - under the "jurisdiction" of and subservient to the Federal Government

The same Senator who was so instrumental in the creation of the Federal Reserve, Nelson Aldrich, also played a key role in the passage of the 16th Amendment, which ushered in our current, 100% unconstitutional income tax fraud! It is worth noting that Aldrich was not only a long-time close associate of the Rothschilds, but that his daughter, Abby Greene Aldrich, also married John D. Rockefeller, Jr. (their son was Nelson A. Rockefeller).

By the end of 1913, the international banking conspiracy not only had the power (through the Federal Reserve) to control the nation's money supply, and loan infinite amounts of money to governments at interest rates dictated solely by the conspirators themselves (not only to the U.S. government, but also to foreign governments - without the consent of the American people), but it also now had the "legal" (though completely unconstitutional) means with which to force U.S. citizens to pay these so-called "loans" back!! This was - and is - no more than "legalized" plunder!

Frederick Bastiat, author *of The Law,* explains what the power to steal from (tax) the people means: "But how is this legal plunder to be identified? Quite simply...see if the law takes from some persons what belongs to them, and gives it to other persons to whom it does not belong! See if the law benefits one citizen at the expense of another by doing what the citizen himself cannot do without committing a crime!" This is an extremely accurate explanation of what had been accomplished with the passage of the graduated income tax!

World War I and the Presidency of Woodrow Wilson

"I have betrayed my country!" - Woodrow Wilson

Ask the average person, "What started World War IT' and you will probably get no more than a blank stare. Even most history professors when asked this question will be at a loss for words, or at best mumble some confusing gibberish about the assassination of Archduke Ferdinand of Austria... As a result of Ferdinand's assassination, Austria demanded an apology from Serbia (the country in which Ferdinand was killed), and Serbia gave them one. Nevertheless, Austria declared war on Serbia anyway, and the other nations of Europe, which had no stake in the dispute, soon also entered the war. This was accomplished by the conspiracy through intense, subversive "hate" propaganda administered discretely at the upper levels of governments on both sides of the so-called "conflict" - which would never have even existed without the instigation of the international banking conspiracy!

It is not a coincidence that World War I started just one year after the creation of the Federal Reserve! The European nations were all nearly broke because they had been arming themselves heavily for several years prior to the war. This was due to the hate propaganda against all factions, which was induced by infiltrators from the banking conspiracy, with the intent of throwing the entire continent into war, so the bankers could profit from all sides! As a result, the European governments had to borrow twenty-five billion dollars from the central bank of the U.S. (or more accurately, the conspiratorial creation of the Federal Reserve), which they did with neither the knowledge nor consent of the American people until after the fact! These debts were never paid back; because they were initially made through Rothschild controlled European banks, which *purposely defaulted* on the loans - whether or not the European governments repaid the issuing European banks! These debts were therefore passed on to the citizens of the United States (as usual)!

In other words, the banking conspiracy, acting through the Federal Reserve, lent huge sums of *American money* to foreign governments (through the conspiracy's own foreign banks) - without the consent of the American people, then whether or not they received repayment of the loans from those governments, the conspirators (through their foreign banks) defaulted on the loans from the Federal Reserve, claiming inability to repay due to not having received any repayment from the various governments, so the American people would have to "pay off' the foreign loans again!! To fully understand this thievery of American property, let us use an analogy:

Imagine that you lend money your favorite Aunt, supposedly to help one of her friends. Now imagine that the friend repays the loan in full to your Aunt, but she doesn't tell you this. Instead, she says that her friend couldn't pay her back the money, so she asks you to pay it back for her friend, which you do! In other words, she asks you to pay back your own money to her, which she *borrowed from you to begin with,* instead of offering to pay you your money back, as she should! Would you agree to such a preposterous arrangement? Of course not! But that's exactly what happened in World War I to the American people at the hands of the unscrupulous bankers...

This formula of outright extortion worked so well (thanks to their blatant lies, double-talk, and deceit) that the banking conspiracy has used this very same formula continuously and without fail at every opportunity - over and over again against the American people (in every ensuing war, every minor conflict, and every other loan for any purpose whatsoever to any foreign power - even unto this day! This is the reason why the United States jumps in and lends money to literally everyone on earth at the drop of a hat, while many Americans right here at home are starving or being forced out of their homes and onto the streets (which is exactly what the bankers want!)

In this despicable, ruthless, and unspeakably criminal way, American citizens have been forced, without their knowledge or consent, to lend to foreign governments (read that "foreign banking interests", also under control of the banking conspiracy). Then (often falsely) claiming that the loans were never repaid, they extorted the same amount (which wasn't theirs to begin with) *again* from the American people... "Why would they do this?" you might ask. Because - beyond reaping incredible profits, not only once or twice, but also sometimes *three times - their* main objective was to destroy the United States of America, whose Constitution was an unbearable threat to their plan of world domination.

With the power to create money out of nothing and collect interest on it through the Federal Reserve, all the banking conspiracy needed was a reason to lend enormous sums of money. World War I gave them that reason... In fact, without the Federal Reserve, World War I might not have been fought, because there would have been no way to fund the war... And without the interference and manipulation of the banking cartel into the internal affairs of the European governments, there would never have been any reason for a war to begin with!

Another means of paying for the war, the graduated income tax (unconstitutionally and fraudulently imposed on American citizens, as we shall soon see) "just happened" to have been created in *the nick of time!* Cordell Hull, whose *Memoirs* shed valuable insight into the treachery and deceit of the conspiracy, had this observation:

"The conflict (World War 1) forced the further development of the income-tax principle. Aiming, as it did, at the one great-untaxed source of revenue, the income-tax law had been created in the nick of time to meet the demands of war. And the conflict also assisted the putting into effect of the Federal Reserve System, likewise in the nick of time." To even the most casual observer, World War I was purposely instigated only after the instruments were in place which assured the bankers of reaping the highest possible profit: the Federal Reserve and the graduated income tax!

Now at last the international banking conspirators had a central bank with which to make loans and collect interest, a locked-in source of numerous borrowers of huge loans (due to the world war), and a means of forcing the American people to foot the bill for all of the loans - both coming and going!

Interestingly, Max Warburg, brother of Paul Warburg (chief drafter of the Federal Reserve Act, principle of Kuhn Loeb Bank - one of the owners of the Federal Reserve, and highly paid associate of the Rothschilds), was the head of the German Secret Service. Max was also the personal banker for Kaiser Wilhelm, and a leading member of the dominant German news agency, Wolff - which was owned by the Rothschilds! Kaiser Wilhelm used the Wolff news agency to agitate the Germans to the degree that they were eager for World War 1. Max Warburg then secured funding for the Kaiser's war effort, while his brother Paul, through his bank and the Federal Reserve, funded the opposition to the Kaiser... All this while the Rothschilds sat quietly watching - and smiling - in the background. Are you beginning to detect a pattern here? I hope so, because twenty years later under Hitler, the exact same pattern was repeated, (although enormously magnified) by the bankers - with the help of DNB, successor to Wolff!

To pull all of this off, the conspirators needed a "yes man" in the White House. They knew that if Robert Taft were to win the presidential election, their plans would be ruined. So they manipulated the election by backing Theodore Roosevelt as a third candidate, who they knew would take votes away from Taft. Their plan worked, and Woodrow

Wilson won the election. With Wilson in the White House, the conspirators had complete control...

Woodrow Wilson was not really President at all. He was no more than a pawn, totally under the thumb of his closest advisor, Colonel Edward Mandell House. House was a key player in the creation of the Federal Reserve. He also assisted in channeling funds to the Bolsheviks for their revolution in Russia, was a strong supporter of the U.S. joining the League of Nations, and organized the creation of the Council on Foreign Relations, and the Royal Institute on International Affairs. House had close ties with the Rothschilds and was an avid believer in a one-world government. He even remarked in his writings that he was seeking "Socialism as dreamed of by Karl Marx."

Wilson himself said, "Mr. House is my second personality. He is my independent self. His thoughts and mine are one. If I were in his place I would do just as he suggested... If anyone thinks he is reflecting my opinions by whatever actions he takes, the are welcome to the conclusion." Arthur Smith, in his 1918 biography of House said that House "holds a power never wielded before in this country by any man out of office - a power greater than that of any political boss or Cabinet member."

In other words, with Wilson acting merely as a mouthpiece for House, we had a President who wanted to establish Communism as "dreamed of by Karl Marx." Actually, as previously mentioned, the Communist Manifesto was not written by Karl Marx, but was actually Amschel Rothschild's plan for world domination. Karl Marx's name did not even appear on any copies of the manifesto for more than twenty years after it was written!

Wilson was re-elected on the slogan "He kept us out of war." In true international banking conspiracy fashion, this was a blatant lie. Ten months before the election, which returned Wilson to the White House in 1916, Colonel House negotiated a secret agreement with England and France on behalf of the Allies! Unknown to the American people, it was already planned that America would participate in the war!

The alleged reason America became involved in World War 1, was that a German submarine torpedoed the British ship, the Lusitainia, which was carrying American passengers. Unknown to most people outside the conspiracy, however, it was also carrying a stockpile of munitions headed for England (Germany's enemy). These munitions 'just happened' to have been produced by a factory owned by J.P. Morgan, who was one of the international conspirators. Also, the Lusitainia was sent without her escorts at considerably reduced speed into an area where a U-boat was known to be waiting! The sinking of the Lusitainia and America's subsequent entrance into the war was, as usual, a set-up from beginning to end!

At the end of the war, the Treaty of Versailles was designed at the Paris Peace Conference with the sole intention of creating as much turmoil in Europe as possible. The impositions on Germany were so extreme that they could not help but create a situation ripe for the rise of someone like Hitler... Even though World War I was called "the war to end all wars," it would have been more accurate to call it "the war to start more wars!" Realizing this, Lord Curzon of England said, "This is no peace. This is only a truce for twenty years." Even conspirator John Maynard Keynes said, "This peace is outrageous and impossible, and can bring nothing but misfortune behind it."

After the Treaty of Versailles was signed, the harsh war reparations included in the treaty ravaged the economy of Germany. In attempting to pay off the war debt, hyperinflation was rampant. This was intensified by the practices of the Federal Reserve, which threw the weight of its influence toward the policy of extreme inflation of the German Mark. The international banking cartel wanted chaos in post war Germany, in order to create a situation ripe for later wars and exploitation.

Thanks to intensive meddling from the banking cartel, the German economy almost collapsed entirely. It was rescued "in the nick of time" by the Dawes plan (created by the banking conspiracy), which was supposed to stabilize the situation and "assist" Germany in paying the war debts. As usual, the Dawes plan was set up to reap substantial profits for the bankers through countless loans.

One of the primary companies to receive "assistance" from the Dawes plan was the I.G. Farben company, which 'just happened' to be headed by Paul Warburg... and also which became one of the most important supply companies to Hitler! In any case, Germany was purposely left in shambles at the end of World War I - both through the Versailles "peace" treaty, and from the economic "assistance" provided by the West. This fact is even acknowledged by our establishment published school textbooks, which also cite this turmoil as the cause for Hitler's rise to power.

To summarize Woodrow Wilson's Presidency: he signed into effect the Federal Reserve and the graduated income tax; he made secret agreements (through Edward Mandell House) with England and France to get America into war; he lied to the American people about almost everything that happened during his terms in office; and he was all the while in the back pocket of the conspiracy. Despite all of this, he must have felt some remorse about what he had done, because he wrote." There is a power somewhere so organized, so subtle, so watchful, so interlocked, so complete, so pervasive - that they better not, speak above their breath when they speak in condemnation of it." He also said, "We have come to be one of the most completely controlled and dominated governments in the world - no longer a government of free opinion, no longer a government by conviction and vote of the majority, but a government by the opinion and duress of small groups of dominant men."

Wilson without doubt contributed greatly to the destruction of America, committing acts of high treason against the American people. If it is difficult to understand his motives, it is almost impossible to forgive him! ... He seemed to know this, because on his deathbed he said, "I have betrayed my country!"

Meanwhile, the conspirators had been hard at work, laying more groundwork for their eventual worldwide dictatorship. As we have learned, World War I was fought by both the European countries and the U.S., due to the "crisis" the conspiracy created. Without their sinister influence, the war would never have been fought. They created the war in order to collect huge profits from both sides, to strengthen their grasp over the world, and to set the stage for yet another, even more costly and horrifying war. But before they could instigate World War 11, they needed to establish an international political body, which they could slowly expand in power and authority until it became the backbone of their "New World Order" dictatorship...

The League of Nations and the Council on Foreign Relations

'...An end-run around national sovereignty, eroding it piece by piece, will accomplish much more than the old-fashioned frontal assault. " - Richard Gardner,

The League of Nations was ratified on January 10th, 1920, and was signed by - whom else? - President ("Puppet" would have been a more fitting title!) Wilson, of course! The League of Nations was supposedly an international organization, created with the intention of promoting international relations and preventing further wars. In reality, it was the first attempt at creating a world government.

The U.S_ Senate, however, did not think that joining the League would be a good idea, so they voted it down. The United States' refusal to join the League of Nations was a tremendous embarrassment for the conspirators. It meant that their first attempt to unite the world into a one-world government had failed. But they realized that the reason they had failed was because they had tried to move too quickly - and too openly. The conspirators decided that they needed an organization, which could implement world government through patient "gradualism" - or by making seemingly insignificant changes subtly, slowly and steadily, until they had what they wanted without alerting the people to what they were doing. They figured that by the time the American citizens realized what had happened, it would be too late... and they were right!

To accomplish their goal, the conspirators created the "Council on Foreign Relations" (or "CFR"), a very innocent sounding name for a very sinister organization! For maximum protection and effectiveness, even the "CFR" was created through the principle of gradualism...

First, the conspirators created an organization called the Round Table, which was formed by Lord Milner, an agent of the Rothschilds, and the principle trustee of the Cecil

Rhodes fortune (after Rhodes' death). This group was later transformed by Colonel House, John Maynard Keynes, Arnold Toynbee, John Foster Dulles and others into a publicly acknowledged, formal council know as the Institute of International Affairs. Later, in 1921, it was decided that this council was to be broken into an American branch, the CFR, and a British branch, the Royal Institute for International affairs (RIIA). It is members of these groups that currently control the media, tax-exempt foundations such as the Rockefeller, Ford and Carnegie Foundations, all major universities, and all government agencies.

According to the "President's Report," published on August 31st, 1972: "The origins of the Council on Foreign Relations lay in the concern of the founders at what they regarded as the disappointing conduct of the Versailles negotiations, and at the short-sighted (as they saw it) rejection by the United States of membership in the League of Nations. In 1921 they founded the Council as a privately funded, nonprofit and nonpartisan organization of individual members."

The CFR pushed for a global government from day one. In fact, the CFR did not waste any time getting to its objective. The first issue of its mouthpiece magazine, *Foreign Affairs* (long considered by both Washington insiders and "wanna-be", to be THE publication to read), had an article entitled "The Next American contribution to Civilization." The article said "Our government should enter heartily into the existing League [of Nations], and be ready to take more than its share in all the responsibilities which unanimous action of the nations constituting the League might impose." (H)

CFR member Allen Dulles laid out the goals for the CFR, saying: "There is no indication that American public opinion for example, would approve the establishment of a super state, or permit American membership in it. In other word time -a *long* time - will be needed before world government is politically feasible... This time element might seeming be shortened so far as American opinion is concerned, by an active propaganda campaign in this country."

From a CFR publication entitled Public *Opinion and Postwar Security Commitments,* we see another example of t Council on Foreign Relations' opinion toward national sovereignty verses world government: " The sovereignty fetish is still so strong in the public mind, that there would appear to be little chance of winning popular assent to American membership in anything approaching a super-state organization. Much will depend on the kind of approach which is u in further popular *education."* (Read that last word as "brainwashing"...!)

Over the years the influence of the CFR has grown significantly to the point where it now controls all of the media most of the U.S. government. In fact, it has become so powerful the *Time* magazine (owned by CFR conspirators) c~ *Foreign Affairs* "the most influential periodical in print."

This tremendous power in the hands of the conspirators' Council on Foreign Relations is anything but good! A former member of the CFR, Rear Admiral Chester Ward, explained in 1980 the intentions of this organization: "The powerful clique [in the CFRJ has one objective... they want to bring about the surrender of the sovereignty an national independence of the United States.

"The second clique of *international (!)* members of the CFR are comprised of the Wall Street international bankers and agents. Primarily, they want the world banking monopoly from whatever power ends up in control of the government. They would probably prefer that this be an all-powerful United Nations organization, but they are prepared to deal with and for a one-world government controlled by the Soviet Communists, if the U.S. Sovereigns, ever surrendered to them."

As you can see, the members of the CFR are not concerned with the best interests of the United States, or an, country. They are seeking total power!

It is important to note that the CFR is not THE conspiracy; it is merely a surface element of it. The congressional reports of February 9th, 1917, explains: "The CFR, as such, does not write the platforms of both political parties or buy off, respective presidential candidates, or control U.S. defense and foreign policies. But CFR members, as individual: in concert with other CFR members, do."

Another U.S. Congressman, John R. Rarick, had this to say about the CFR: "The Council on Foreign Re dedicated to one-world government, financed by a number of the largest tax-exempt foundations, and wielding supreme power, and influence over our lives in the areas of finance, business, labor, military, education, and mass communication should be familiar to every member [of Congress] concerned with good government, and with preserving and (the Constitution and our free-enterprise system. Yet the nation's right-to-know machinery, the news media (is aggressive in exposures to inform our people) remain conspicuously silent when it comes to the CFR, its members, and their activities. And I find that few university students and graduates have even *heard of* the Council on Foreign Relations. The CFR is 'the establishment.' Not only does it have the influence and power in key decision-making positions at the highest levels of government to apply pressure from above, but it also finances and uses individuals and groups to bring pressure from below, to justify the high level decisions for converting the United States from a sovereign Constitutional Republic into a servile member state of a one-world dictatorship."

The CFR also has close relations with the United Nations, which could be said to be an even larger part of the conspiracy for world government than the CFR is. The UN, like the League of Nations before it, is the transition stage from national sovereignty to one-world government. The goals of both the CFR and the UN are amazingly similar, and seem to work together.

One of the founders of the CFR was John Foster Dulles, who was later appointed Secretary of State by CFR member, President Dwight Eisenhower a was very surprised to learn that "Ike" was involved in all this!) In 1939, Dulles laid out part of the conspiracy's plan for the world:

"Some dilution or leveling of the sovereignty system as it prevails in the world today must take place... to the immediate disadvantage of those nations which now possess the preponderance of power... The establishment of a common money... would deprive our government of exclusive control over a national money... The United States must be prepared to make sacrifices afterward in setting up a world politico-economic order, which would level off inequalities of economic opportunity with respect to nations." ["Dulles Outlines World Peace Plan," *New York Times,* October 28th, 1939]

In his meticulous expose of the Federal Reserve, *The Creature From Jekyll Island,* G. Edward Griffin sums up the CFR: "The CFR, which was initially dominated by J.P. Morgan and later by the Rockefellers, is the most powerful group in America today. It is even more powerful than the federal government, because almost all the key positions in the government are held by its members. In other words, it is the United States government!"

In other words, the CFR wields tremendous power, and is one of the key organizations in creating one-world government. It was founded out of the failure of the League of Nations, which itself would have been the first step toward world government, much like the UN is today. However powerful it may be, the CFR is only one surface element of a much larger and more powerful organization -

the international banking conspiracy itself. Eliminating the CFR's influence would not really solve anything, as it would soon be replaced by another similar structure to do the conspiracy's bidding.

The Bolshevik Revolution and the Rise of Communism

"The ultimate purpose of all income redistribution is people control. Trotsky

While some of the conspirators were hard at work in the United States establishing the Federal Reserve, implementing the graduated income tax, and laying the groundwork for World War 1, other conspirators were laboring patiently and diligently toward the initial implementation of Amschel Rothschild's plan for world domination... The American people still clung too strongly to their ideas of liberty and sovereignty, and were not yet even close to being ready for their master plan'. Likewise, Europeans - although beset with regional differences, and thus ripe for massive exploitation (as evidenced by the relatively simple instigation of World War I) - had far too much nationalistic and ethnic pride to be herded into any type of 'super-state' political system... The orient, on the other hand, was politically and ethnically, and (most importantly) economically too far removed from western philosophy and culture for the conspirators to manipulate... Africa was too diverse and undeveloped to make such an attempt even remotely profitable... India was too poor, and still under heavy influence of the deteriorating British Empire...

Still there existed one country - very close to European in background and culture (increasing ease of infiltration), with almost unlimited natural resources (making it a very tantalizing target), and on the verge of casting off the chains of one of the last of the great western-style empires, rendering it politically unstable (and thus easier to manipulate). These factors combined made this country the perfect initial testing ground for Amschel's plan of world domination (as defined by the conspiracy's 1848 publication, *"The Communist Manifesto."* The target country was, of course, Russia! According to our history books (published by the conspiracy-controlled major publishing houses) the Bolshevik Revolution of 1917 was a grass-roots revolt to throw off the shackles of the Czar. Although it is true that the Russian people wanted reform, and that there was an upheaval, they in no way wanted what they got with the Bolsheviks - which merely resulted in replacing one feudal system with another.

The truth is that there were, actually two revolutions in 1917 Russia. The first revolution took place in February, which resulted in the establishment of a provisional socialist government under the leadership of Aleksandr Kerensky. This government was relatively mild in its policies, and attempted to accommodate all factions, including the Bolsheviks, who were in the minority... It is important to realize that when this first revolution took place, *neither Lenin nor Trotsky were even in Russia!*

A second revolution took place a few short months later, called 'the October Revolution,' which brought the Bolsheviks to power. This second revolution was essentially a coup d'etat, financed by the international banking conspiracy. Contrary to Marxism myth, this revolution was not a 'people's rebellion', but an insurrection of the radical Bolshevik minority who 'just happened' to have the guns and the money for bribes and propaganda necessary to insure their victory.

Congressman Louis McFadden, a true patriot, and a man of unusual insight, honesty and courage (and about whom you *will never* read in our conspiracy-controlled history and text books!), was Chairman of the House Banking

Committee at that time. He went on record as saying: "They [the international banking conspiracy] financed Trotsky's mass meetings of the "discontented and rebellious" in New York. They paid Trotsky's passage from New York to Russia so that he might assist in the destruction of the Russian empire. They tormented and instigated the Russian Revolution, and they placed a large fund of American dollars at Trotsky's disposal in one of their branch banks in Sweden.."

Once the Bolsheviks were in power, the middle class (or the 'grass roots' who initially revolted in February) was destroyed when the Bolsheviks nationalized everything, supposedly in the name of the 'people.' It is also interesting to note that after the Bolsheviks took control, all the banks were "nationalized" except one: the Petrograd branch of the Rockefeller's National City Bank... All of the banks, which were "nationalized", were not run by the state, but rather by private, international bankers!

It is obvious, then, that the October Revolution was not "of the people" at all, but rather a timely grab for power by a small minority (the Bolsheviks), who wanted totalitarian control, and who were funded by the international banking conspiracy! The conspiracy got two things out of this: first, they gained control over a massive percent of the earth; and second, they now had the perfect country to use as a 'nemesis' for the U.S., so they could apply the Rothschild Formula ("pit two sides against each other, and profit from both sides"). Russia was to become "the best enemy (of the U.S.) money could buy!"

After the October Revolution, Russia was very weak. It lost 40 million of its population during the Revolution, followed by another 66 million killed by the Bolsheviks! The Bolshevik regime was saved from certain collapse, and Lenin was able to consolidate his power and control over all of Russia only because conspiracy puppet, President Woodrow Wilson, shipped 700,000 tons of American food (which should have gone to feed Americans!) to the fledgling Soviet Union.

In fact, Wilson, who was - just as the Bolsheviks were - employed by the international banking conspiracy, had this to say about the Bolshevik Revolution: "Assurance has been added to our hope for the future peace of the world, by the wonderful and heartening things that have been happening in the last few weeks in Russia. Here is a fit partner for the League of Honor." He was saying this of a "revolution" that installed as the absolute dictator of Russia, Lenin - a man who slaughtered millions! Less than two years later, Wilson sent Elcho Root to Russia with $20 million U.S. tax dollars! It 'just happened' that Root was an attorney for Kuhn Loeb Bank (one of the owners of the Federal Reserve!), and a former Secretary of State! This money was supposedly designated as part of a U.S. war fund... proving that U.S. money was going to the support of the Bolshevik regime.

Lenin himself confirmed this when he said, `The Capitalists of the world and their governments, in pursuit of conquest of the Soviet market, will close their eyes to the indicated higher reality [that the bankers were the ones really in control of both the U.S. and the U.S.S.R.], and thus will turn into deaf-mute blind men. They will extend credits, which will strengthen for us the Communist Party in their countries. By giving us the materials and technology we lack, they will restore our military industry, indispensable for our future victorious attack on our suppliers. In other words, they will labor for the preparation of their own suicide."

To Americans who lived most of their lives under the supposed 'threat' of Soviet aggression (especially after World War 11 until the so-called 'demise of Communism' beginning in 1989), it will come as quite a shock that the USSR was never really a valid military threat... It was just made to appear that way. Thus the international banking conspiracy used it to apply the Rothschild formula of pitting one country against another, so the bankers could make huge profits on both sides, while moving the entire planet closer to their vision of a one-world dictatorship! The fact is, the conspiracy funded and built the USSR largely from American money, stolen from Americans through the Federal Reserve and the IRS!

In addition to funding from the US, the Bolsheviks relied heavily on funding from the international banking conspiracy. Russian General Arsene de Goulevitch revealed the connection between the Bolsheviks and the Wall Street bankers, saying: "Mr. Bakmetiev, the late Russian Imperial Ambassador to the United Sates, tells us that the Bolsheviks, after their victory, transferred 600 million rubles in gold between the years 1918-1922 to Kuhn-Loeb Company [one of the owners of the Federal Reserve]."

The director of the Federal Reserve at the time, William B. Thompson, gave $20 million to the Bolsheviks. This was very easy for him to do, because he was in a position of great power as the Federal Reserve director, but also because he held major interests in the Chase National Bank (controlled by the Rockefellers. Don't forget, the Rockefellers- 'just happened' to have the only bank in Russia which was not nationalized... Even though the $20 million Thompson gave to the Bolsheviks (never expecting or receiving repayment) belonged to the American people, Thompson was also generous enough to donate $1 million of his 'own'(?) money to the Bolsheviks for the purpose of spreading their doctrine in Germany and Austria.

To disguise their funding to the Bolsheviks, the banking conspirators organized the "Red Cross" (does the name "Rosicrucian" ring a bell?), through which various agents and associates of the bankers doled out large sums of money to Russians, usually right before they 'just happened' to revolt and join the ranks of the Bolsheviks! J.P. Morgan himself contributed $100,000... And according to his own grandson, John, Jacob Schiff "sunk about $20 million for the triumph of Bolshevism in Russia. Other New York banking firms also contributed." ...By the way, William B. Thompson was the head of the American Red Cross mission in Moscow!

The head of the American Red Cross mission in St. Petersburg (Petrograd) was Raymond Robins. It 'just happened' that he had also been a leading figure in Teddy Roosevelt's "Bull Moose" campaign for the American Presidency in 1912! Although a wealthy man, he was a staunch anti-capitalist, and an avid supporter of one-world government and the international banking conspiracy. (It is interesting to note that one of Raymond Robin's idols was none other than Rothschild agent, Cecil Rhodes.)

Robins was also fascinated by Lenin, and became the only man whom Lenin was always willing to see, and who ever succeeded in imposing his own personality on the unemotional Bolshevik leader... As a result, Robins became the main intermediary between the Bolsheviks and the American government, and was largely responsible for persuading President Woodrow Wilson to give diplomatic recognition to the Soviet regime.

The Great Depression and the Presidency of Franklin D. Roosevelt

"The international bankers sought to bring about a condition of despair here, so that they might emerge as rulers of us all!' - Louis McFadden

While the conspirators (through the Bolsheviks and in the name of Communism) were tightening their hold on the Russian people, and gearing up for their more-than-eighty-years of iron-fisted despotism, they were also hard at work elsewhere: paving the way for a socialist government here in the United States; and preparing Europe for the biggest and most destructive war ever - World War 11.

The conspiracy, who own controlling interests in both the media and in the major publishing houses which print our history books, all depict the cause of the Great Depression as massive economic speculation and a failure in the free market... In addition, they credit President Franklin D. Roosevelt for bringing the U.S. out of the Depression. Both of these "truths" are outright lies!

The real truth is that the conspirators used the power of the Federal Reserve to expand the money supply dramatically. In 1922 the amount of money in circulation was approximately $33 billion dollars. The amount was increased every year until by 1928 there was more than $45.7 billion dollars in circulation (that additional $12.7 billion dollars being that much more "debt" the American citizens supposedly "owed" to the Fed - plus interest, of course!)... This period of "easy money" caused massive speculation in the private sector - just as anticipated by the conspirators, who then ordered the Federal Reserve to withdraw money from circulation... as quickly as they determined the economy could bear without collapsing it entirely (which they knew could bring on a revolution from the people). By 1933 there was only $30 billion in circulation, and America was brought to her knees!

As one of the few brave enough to be an outspoken critic of the conspiracy, Congressman Charles Lindbergh wrote: "Under the Federal Reserve, panics are scientifically created. The present panic is the first scientifically created one, worked out as we might figure a mathematical problem."

The hard times that followed created unspeakable suffering for all Americans except the very wealthy (mostly, the conspirators themselves!). Many families never recovered from the disaster. If anyone reading this knows or is related to anyone who went through this horrible period (and I bet that would be practically *everybody* who is reading this report), just consider this: 'Me hardships, despair, and misery that your family or loved ones (or even you, if you were alive at the time) suffered during the Depression didn't "just happen," and were not the result of some uncontrollable force of fate or destiny, but were meticulously planned and purposely caused to turn our American Republic into socialist state! This was done by the same despicable group of criminals who have since stolen practically all our property, our rights, our freedom, and our privacy... and who fully intend to continue to take everything we have until we are forced to give up the last vestiges of our sovereignty to become mere slaves to their one-world dictatorship!

Another true patriot and critic of the Federal Reserve who saw through the conspiracy's plan, Congressman Louis McFadden, was still Chairman of the House Banking Committee at the time. He had this to say about the Depression: "It was not accidental. It was a carefully contrived occurrence. The international bankers sought to bring about a condition of despair here so that they might emerge as rulers of us all!"

Curtis Dail, FDR's son-in-law, who also "just happened" to be a manager for Lehman Brothers (one of the owners of the Federal Reserve - what a surprise!) was on the floor of the New York Stock Exchange the day of the Crash. He said, "Actually, it was a calculated 'shearing' of the public by the world money powers, triggered by the planned sudden shortage of call money in the New York money market."

William Bryon, author *of The United States' Unsolved Monetary and Political Problems,"* had this to say regarding the Panic of 1929: "When everything was ready, the New York financiers started calling 24 hour broker call loans. This meant that the stockbrokers and the customers had to dump their stock on the market in order to pay the loans. This naturally collapsed the stock market, and brought a banking collapse all over the country, because the banks not owned by the oligarchy were heavily involved in broker call claims at this time. Bank runs soon exhausted their coin and currency, and they had to close. The Federal Reserve refused to come to their aid, even though they were instructed under the law to maintain an elastic currency."

Not all members of the U.S. government had been bought off or brainwashed by the conspiracy. Those who tried to tell the American people the truth, however, were usually intimidated, coerced, threatened - or silenced - to send a message to any other public figure that might oppose them! These gangster tactics worked very well on most members of the government... But not on Congressman Louis McFadden!

As chairman of the House Banking and Currency Committee for more than 10 years, Louis McFadden understood exactly what the Federal Reserve was, who controlled it, and what they were up to! On June 10th, 1932, Congressman McFadden fearlessly stood up before

Congress and bravely challenged the Federal Reserve in the following powerful speech:

"Mr. Chairman, we have in this country one of the most corrupt institutions the world has ever known. I refer to the Federal Reserve Board and the Federal Reserve banks, which have cheated the government and the people of the United States out of enough money to pay the national debt several times over. This evil institution has impoverished and ruined the people of the United States, and has practically bankrupted our government. It has done this through the defects of the law under which it operates, through the maladministration of that law, by the Federal Reserve Board, and through the corrupt practices of the moneyed vultures who control it!

"Some people think the Federal Reserve banks are United States government institutions. *They are* NOT! They are private credit monopolies, which prey upon the people of the United States for the benefit of themselves and their foreign swindlers, and the rich and predatory moneylenders. In that dark crew of financial pirates, there are those who would cut a man's throat to get a dollar out of his pocket; there are those who send money into states to buy votes to control our legislation; and there are those who maintain international propaganda for the purpose of deceiving us and wheedling us into granting new concessions which will permit them to cover up their past misdeeds and set again in motion their gigantic train of crime!

"These twelve private credit monopolies were deceitfully and disloyally foisted upon this Country by bankers who came here from Europe, and repaid our hospitality by undermining our American institutions. Those bankers took money out of this Country to finance Japan in a war against Russia. They created a reign of terror in Russia with our money. They planned and instigated the Russian Revolution...

"In 1912 the National Monetary Association, under the chairmanship of the late Senator Nelson Aldrich, presented a vicious bill called the National Reserve Association Bill. This is usually spoken of as the Aldrich bill, although Aldrich did not write it. He was the tool, if not the accomplice, of the European bankers who, for nearly 20 years, had been scheming to set up a central bank in America. In 1912 they were spending - and are continuing to spend vast sums of money to accomplish their purpose.

"We were opposed to the Aldrich plan for a central bank. The men who ruled the Democratic Party then promised the people that if they were returned to power there would be no central bank established here while they held the reigns of government. Thirteen months later, that promise was broken, and the Wilson administration, under the tutelage of sinister Wall Street figures, established, here in our free Country, the worm-eaten monarchical institution of the 'King's Bank' - to control us from the top downward, and to shackle us from the cradle to the grave!

"When the Federal Reserve Act was passed, the people of these United States did not perceive that a world banking system was being set up here... A super-state, controlled by international bankers and international industries acting together to enslave the world for their own pleasure. *Every effort has been made by the Federal Reserve Board to conceal its powers, but the truth is: The Fed has usurped the government! It controls everything here, and it controls all our foreign relations! It makes or breaks governments at will!*"

The near collapse of the economy due to the contraction of the money supply led to a public outcry for government intervention. Herbert Hoover was blamed for the Depression (although in reality he had absolutely nothing to do with id), and was ousted from office by conspiracy-backed Franklin D. Roosevelt. This public outcry (greatly inflamed by the media) was exactly what the conspiracy had been trying to create as the perfect opportunity for them to institute even more of the socialistic programs that had already been laid out by Colonel Edward Mandell House.

It is important to be aware of the fact that Roosevelt (FDR) was nearly as close to House as Wilson was. This fact is amply demonstrated in a letter Roosevelt wrote House, describing the nature of the banking conspiracy's control: "The real truth of the matter is, as you and I know, that a financial element in the larger centers has owned the government ever since the days of Andrew Jackson..."

Although it was the banking cartel of the U.S. (die Federal Reserve and its owners) that orchestrated the Great Depression, it was ultimately directed by the international banking conspiracy, particularly the Rothschild family. In *Secrets of the Federal Reserve,* Eustace Mullins provides evidence of the shadowy Rothschild control:

"On February 6th, 1929, Mr. Montague Norman, governor of the bank of England [and an agent of the Rothschilds, came to Washington and had a conference with Andrew Mellon, Secretary of the Treasury. Immediately after that mysterious visit, the Federal Reserve Board abruptly changed its policy and pursued a high discount rate policy, abandoning the cheap money policy which it had inaugurated in 1927, after Mr. Norman's other visit. The stock market crash and the deflation of the American people's financial structure were scheduled to take place in March. To get the ball rolling, Paul Warburg gave the official warning to the traders to get out of the market."

So, the Depression was caused by the bankers - that much is obvious to even the most naive observer... But how did President Roosevelt fit into this picture...?

Contrary to popular history (as edited and controlled by the conspiracy), President Roosevelt was no saint. Since we have seen that the Depression was created by - and ended by - the bankers, what role did Roosevelt play? It was the role of the 'leading man'. Here's what really happened...

THE END

To begin with, Roosevelt's son-in-law, Curtis Dail, wrote: "For a long time I felt that FDR had developed many thoughts and ideas that were his own, to benefit this country. But he didn't. Most of his thoughts, his political 'ammunition,' as it were, were carefully manufactured for him in advance by the CFR/one-world money group. Brilliantly, with great gusto, like a fine piece of artillery, he exploded that prepared 'ammunition' in the middle of an unsuspecting target, the American people [exactly what happened with Hitler as well!] - and thus paid off and retained his internationalist political support. "

FDR did more than any other person to totally destroy the United States, by setting himself up as a totalitarian dictator (and all subsequent presidents since). He did this under the Constitutional "doctrine of emergency," by enacting what is known as "The War Powers Act." True, because of the Great Depression, the United States was in a state of emergency, but it was a condition purposefully created by the conspiracy to gain control of America - and that so-called "emergency" could have been easily relieved through honest banking practices - but the conspirators *wanted* America to be in their intentionally contrived state of near-collapse, so they could seize control! Which is exactly what they did!!

The Corruption of the Legal System and the Courts

"Your court is operating in an Admiralty Jurisdiction. Call it anything you want, but do not call it 'Admiralty!'" - the international banking conspirators to high officials in the U.S. Judicial system, during a secret meeting

In 1933, Congressman James Black stated in the *Congressional Record:* "If I think of all the damnable heresies that have ever been suggested in connection with the Constitution, the doctrine of emergency is the worst. It means that when Congress declares an emergency, there is no Constitution! This means it's dead!"

When Franklin Delano Roosevelt came to the White House in 1933, the United States was in the midst of the Great Depression. It was considered an emergency...

FDR was inaugurated on March 4th, 1933. On March 5th he issued his first emergency proclamation - #2038. That proclamation called for an extraordinary emergency session of Congress to be convened on March 9th, 1933, at 12 noon. That Congress convened, and passed its first act, entitled "The Emergency Banking Relief Act," which essentially gave FDR the power to issue any regulation, order, license, rule, or proclamation from March 4th, 1933 - or anytime in the future - as conferred under the act of October 6th, 1917.

What does the act of October 6th, 1917 have to do with all this? That is the infamous "Trading With the Enemy" Act, in which German citizens were placed totally under the power of the president of the United States. They were considered 'enemies' of the United States, and because of that, the executive branch of the United States was given total authority over them!

So, when Roosevelt was given authority to act under the 1917 "Trading With the Enemy" act, he essentially was given total, dictatorial control over the entire United States, and all American citizens were considered to be "enemies" (!!!) - and, therefore, under his authority!

In other words, the American people were no longer excluded from the almost unlimited powers granted to Roosevelt in the War Powers Act as approved by Congress on March 9th, 1933! In fact, all of the transactions of the American people were included under the powers of that act! But even worse than the establishment of a dictatorial *war* government (otherwise know as 'martial law'), which authorized the president to do anything that he deemed necessary for the operation of the country, is the horrifying fact that the War Powers Act has never been repealed!

This means that for more than 60 years, the Constitution has been illegally bypassed, and the people of the United States have been living under martial law! But it is worse than that - much worse!

Because of his new dictatorial authority, Roosevelt was able to seize all Constitutional money - including gold and silver owned by private citizens! Emergency war currency began to be issued in lieu of the actual United States dollars. This was the first currency, which was actually based on nothing - and backed only by the debts of the American people. This, of course, created a great dilemma: Once that currency was issued through debt, it became a mathematical impossibility to ever pay back the principal on the currency that was issued, plus the interest due on it. The conspirators knew this. In fact, *they were literally banking on it!*

In a single stroke, Roosevelt managed to subjugate the American people under a totalitarian government, and at the same time destroy what was left of our free economy by ordering the issuance of completely worthless, debt-backed currency. But he wasn't through yet!

With the enactment of the War Powers Act on March 9th, 1933, the states were completely obliterated! In other words, according to this criminal Act, there were no longer any 'sovereign states' comprising the United States. All were totally subjugated to the dictatorship of the totalitarian Federal government (although none of the people, and most of the politicians never were made aware of this 'fact', for fear it would cause an immediate revolution!). However, under the emergency (as created by the conspiracy) government, on June 6th, 1934, the states were permitted to enter into interstate compacts. It was called 'regional government.' Under those interstate compacts, the states actually became corporations... and essentially became sub-corporations of the District of Columbia!

Now the conspirators were getting somewhere! Finally, the former 'sovereign states,' which had (under the Constitution) been superior to the Federal government, were now at last under the complete control of Washington D.C., and thus the international banking conspiracy! All 'Citizens' of the various states were therefore automatically considered citizens of the Federal government - just like the 14th Amendment had been set up 70 years earlier to accomplish!

By now, the conspirators - along with their chief executive hatchet man, Roosevelt - were really smiling. But they knew there was still one more 'link to forge' before America - the former 'Land of the Free' - could be forever bound by the chains of slavery to their totalitarian New World Order! They had to abolish all vestiges of Common Law, on which the Constitution is founded...

This was fairly easily accomplished. Because of his ill-gotten dictatorial powers, Roosevelt was able to ram through Congress the 'Federal Rules of Civil Procedure' Act, wherein a new form of courts were introduced into the United States. These new courts, which were to supersede and replace all existing courts (which until that time had operated under Common Law as decreed by the Constitution) were instructed to operate under martial law, which is essentially the same as international admiralty law. The reasoning behind this was not only because the United States was supposedly in a state of national emergency (which by definition requires martial law), but also because for more than 20 years at that time (it's now more than 80 years!), the United States had been 'completely owned by foreign interests!' This was because the National Debt to the international banking conspiracy through the Federal Reserve, was already more than twice the value of all the property of every man, woman and child in the country (% due to the so-called 'interest' accrued on moneys supposedly 'borrowed' from the international banking conspiracy (i.e. the Federal Reserve) ever since the Federal Reserve Act of 1913.

To divert public attention from what was really going on, the courts were instructed to call the new legal system 'Statutory Law,' (a term coined to fool the public), instead of 'Admiralty Law,' which most certainly would have raised many uncomfortable questions that the conspiracy didn't want to deal with... such as "Why am I being tried under admiralty law??"... "Who is the foreign 'third party' involved?"... "How did this foreign 'third party' (the Federal Reserve) become a party in my private affairs without my knowledge or consent?"

Even though Common Law was officially abolished in the U.S. in 1934 under the Federal Rules of Civil Procedure Act, the Supreme Court didn't transmit the new rules to Congress. Furious over their lack of blind obedience to him, Roosevelt "packed" the Supreme Court with justices who would do his bidding without question... So in 1937 the rules were transmitted to Congress by FDR's newly appointed pro-conspiracy Supreme Court, the American court system was changed, and Common Law was abolished along with all the original Constitutional rights of the American people!

Howard Freeman, a renowned expert in the conning and treasonous conversion of our court system from Common Law to statutory law reveals what a respected judge told him in privacy and strictest confidence (lest the judge's colleagues in the legal world should discover that he had exposed their criminal game to a private citizen!)...

Here's what the judge told Howard...

"In 1938, all the higher judges, the top attorneys and the U.S. attorneys were called into a *secret meeting...* and this is what we were told:

'America is a bankrupt nation - it is completely owned by its creditors. 'Me creditors own the Congress, they own the Executive branch, the Judiciary branch, and they own all the State governments! *Take silent judicial notice of this fact, but never reveal it openly. Your court is operating in an Admiralty Jurisdiction... Call it anything you want, but do not call it Admiralty!'"*

Howard explains further: "The reason they cannot call it Admiralty Jurisdiction is that your defense would be quite different in Admiralty Jurisdiction from your defense under Common Law. In Admiralty, there is no court, which has jurisdiction unless there is a valid international contract in dispute. If you know it is Admiralty Jurisdiction, and they have admitted on the record that you are in an Admiralty Court, you can demand that the international maritime contract,

to which you are supposedly a party, and which you supposedly have breached, be placed into evidence! (No court has Admiralty Jurisdiction unless there is a valid international maritime contract that has been breached!)

"So you say, just innocently like a lamb, 'Well, I never knew that I got involved with an international maritime contract, so I deny that such a contract exists. If this court is taking jurisdiction in Admiralty, then place the contract in evidence, so that I may challenge the validity of the contract.' What they would have to do is place the *national debt* into evidence. They would have to admit that the international bankers own the whole nation, and that we are their slaves!

"But, the bankers, at their secret meeting in 1938, instructed the judges and attorneys that it 'is not expedient at this time' to admit that they own everything and could foreclose on every nation of the world. The reason they don't want to tell everyone that they own everything is that there are still too many privately owned guns out there [especially in the United States]... There are uncooperative armies and other military forces [like the growing militia movement in America]. So, until they can gradually consolidate all armies into a WORLD ARMY [which they have almost accomplished with the UN 'peacekeeping' special forces], and all courts into a single WORLD COURT [which is outlined in the UN Covenant, and signed by 134 countries], it is not 'expedient' to admit the jurisdiction the courts are operating under. (When we understand these things, we realize that there are certain secrets they don't want to admit, and we can use this to our benefit.) Since the courts were instructed not to call it 'Admiralty Jurisdiction', they call it 'Statutory Jurisdiction.'"

It is a well-documented fact that Roosevelt was a creation of Wall Street, and an integral part of the New York banking fraternity. If you bear this in mind, it will help to explain much of what he did during his presidency because, even though he *said* that he was trying to help America's poor (a body largely created by the bankers!), the results of his actions did nothing to elevate the poor to greater income and lifestyles, but rather locked them into an inescapable pit of poverty, dependency, and welfare (at the great expense of the 'working class,' who had to foot all the bills!). Here is just a sampling of his 'good' deeds:

Roosevelt initiated a flurry of socialistic, welfare programs, such as the Agricultural Adjustment Administration, and the National Recovery Act, supposedly to 'offset' the economic problems that were created by the bankers in the first place! As a result of these programs, a large percentage of the population began working for the government. This large expense, in addition to the decline in the tax base due to the depression, created a problem for Roosevelt: How to pay for the new socialism? What he really needed was the ability to inflate the currency to pay for the all the new welfare and socialistic programs... The only way to create that much inflation quickly was to take America off the gold standard a totally unconstitutional act, correctly foreseen by our forefathers as completely removing all value from our money, thus leaving it open to absolute manipulation!

Nevertheless, on April 5th, 1933 (less than a month after he initiated martial law through the War Powers Act), President Roosevelt ordered all Americans to turn their gold bullion and gold coins over to the Federal Reserve banking system!! He did this by executive order - without the approval of Congress, which was a direct violation of the Constitution! I guess he figured that since he was now the dictator of the U.S., the Constitution did not apply to him. He also offered no true compensation for the gold, but in the best 'absolute dictator' style, he threatened to imprison anyone who didn't comply! This was nothing more than out-and-out robbery: "Give us your gold - or ELSE!" Worst of all, he ordered that the gold be turned over to Federal Reserve Banks, instead of to the nearest United States mint or depository! In other words, he forced Americans to give their gold directly to the international banking conspiracy! Does anyone out there reading this still believe Roosevelt was a saint??

It was at this time Congressman Louis McFadden, Chairman of the House Banking Committee, charged that the seizure of gold was "an operation run for the benefit of the international bankers." McFadden was powerful enough to ruin the plot to illegally seize all of America's privately owned gold. As James Warburg, son of Paul Warburg and one of the conspirators himself admitted: "[McFadden] was preparing to break the whole deal when he collapsed at a banquet and died. As two assassination attempts had already been made against him, many suspected poisoning."

On February 2nd, 1934, FDR created the Export-Import bank, which he had absolutely no authority to do, to insure loans made to foreign (including communist) nations, to "increase national trade." This was also supposedly to stimulate the Depression-torn U.S. economy. In reality, the Export-Import Bank was a direct subsidization of big industry, which is exactly what the conspirators wanted. Here's how it works: An American manufacturer wants to sell its products to a foreign country, except that country doesn't have the funds to make the purchase. So the Export-Import Bank steps in and "loans" the money to the country, which in reality goes directly to the manufacturer. The importing country then pays installments on the loan, with the interest on the loan paid by the U.S. government (read that as 'American taxpayers'). If the country ever defaults on the loan, the U.S. government (again, read that as 'American taxpayers') pays off the loan to the Export-Import Bank. Since most of these loans were (and still are) defaulted on, this program was in effect a way to transfer wealth from American citizens to big business...

In order to bring the country out of depression, Roosevelt then borrowed massive amounts of money from the banking conspiracy in the name of the people. The American citizens ended up paying for this for years in the form of interest on the national debt, but they didn't know or care at the time. They just wanted to escape from the economic disaster the bankers had created in the first place!

Gradualism (making constant, very small changes toward the desired goal, to escape detection and to avert suspicion and alarm) is the key element the conspirators have always used against the United States in order to bring about their ultimate goals. FDR - and the conspirators behind him - were masters at using deceptive words and outright fraud to trick the public into believing that they were acting for the good of the nation. Creating the Depression allowed Roosevelt to implement many of the important steps toward the goal of one-world socialism. Norman Thomas, head of the Socialist Party in the U.S. at that time said: "The American people will never knowingly accept Socialism, but under the name of Liberalism, they will adopt every fragment of the Socialist program, until one day America will be a Socialist nation without knowing how it happened."

The bankers did not decide to increase the money supply again until it served their interests. The Depression lasted for many years, and caused great suffering. Contrary to 'popular opinion' (as carefully taught to us by the conspiracycontrolled media and publishing houses) it could have been ended at any time by the very conspirators who brought it on. They chose to prolong the agony of the American citizens for two very important reasons: 1) they (the conspirators) were still setting the stage for World War II, and were not quite prepared yet for that ultimate crime against humanity; and 2) they purposely wanted to 'break the American. spirit', so that the people could be more easily controlled and more readily accept their socialistic agenda. As proof of this second point, consider the following excerpt from the February 1934 issue of New American, which was privately circulated among leading bankers of the day:

"Debts must be collected and loans and mortgages must be foreclosed as soon as possible! When the common people have lost their homes, they will be more docile and easier to govern. People without homes will not quarrel with their lenders. "

Although we are encouraged to believe the World War [I ended the Depression, that is a blatant lie! Since the Fed controlled the money supply, it could have increased it and brought the country our of depression (which they created) at any time, but then, the American citizens might not have been so willing to go to war in their carefully constructed World War II... Having the United States fight in WWII 'just happened' to be in the best interests of the international banking conspiracy... so they increased the money supply again only at that point (after the U.S. had already committed to the war which the bankers created), thus ending the Depression.

In summary, the international banking conspiracy created the Great Depression, not only to profit by buying up all the depressed stocks after the stock market crash, but also to create a reason that would allow socialist Franklin Delano Roosevelt (FDR) to begin programs for the process of gradualist socialism. These programs did more to destroy the American political and economic system than any other previous actions. If Franklin Roosevelt is remembered for nothing else, he should be remembered as the one man who almost single-handedly destroyed all that was good and unique about America, and replaced it with insidious vehicles of demoralization and decay - not only for our economy, but for the human spirit as well! World War II brought us out of the Depression, but this is true only because it is what the bankers wanted!!

World War II

"From the days of Spartucus-Weishaupt to those of Karl Marx, to those of Trotsky... this world-wide conspiracy for the overthrow of civilization has been steadily growing. "
- Winston Churchill

Unlike most wars, World War II seemed to have a real cause: a great global threat named Hitler was rising to power. History (as edited by the conspiracy) neglects to mention, however, that Hitler could never have risen to power had it not been for the circumstances created at the end of World War I... nor does it mention that Hitler was not a lone, ruthless, self-sufficient mad man, but was funded and supported - in fact created - by (who else?) none other than the international banking conspiracy!

After World War 1, the Versailles Treaty purposely left Germany in ruin. This was supposedly to have been alleviated by the Dawes plan, an 'economic recovery' act which gave banking cartel money to Germany, but also gave them U.S. taxpayer money and subsidized (by the U.S government - which really means by the American citizens) loans. Much of this money went to I.G. Farben, a giant industrial engineering company of Germany, whose major financial connection was its American branch, know as American I.G. -which 'just happened' to be headed by Paul Warburg (drafter of the Federal Reserve Act, agent of the Rothschilds, and one of the owners of the Federal Reserve).

Paul's brother, Max Warburg, "just happened" to be head of the German central bank, and was therefore able to channel a considerable amount of money from Paul in New York to Hitler in Germany!

Hitler got tremendous support from both I.G. Farben and

the banking conspiracy of Wall Street, as Anthony Sutton, author of Wall Street *and the Rise of* Hitler, points out: "Without the capital supplied by Wall Street, there would have been no I.G. Farben in the first place, and almost certainly no Adolf Hitler and World War U." Furthermore, Standard Oil, owned by the Rockefeller interests, had a joint venture with I.G. Farben to develop a process to convert coal into oil, which was crucial for Germany's war effort.

This is entirely supported by statistics. In 1943, for example, I.G.Farben produced 100% of Germany's synthetic rubber, 100% of its lubricating oil, and 84% of its explosives! It even manufactured the deadly Zyklon B gas, used to exterminate human beings in Hitler's concentration camps! I.G. Farben also supplied 45% of the election funds used to bring Hitler to power in 1933!

Another interesting note is that the Dulles brothers (legal representatives of Kuhn Loeb Company - one of the owners of the Federal Reserve) met with Hitler on January 4th, 1933, to grant Hitler the funds he needed to become Chancellor of Germany... By the way, one of the brothers - John Foster Dulles - later became" Secretary of State to Eisenhower!

Additional assistance was given to Hitler in the early part of his rise to power by the Bank of England itself (controlled by the Rothschilds). Biographer John- Hargrave revealed, "It is quite certain that Mr. Norman [head of the Bank of England at that time] did all he could to assist Hitlerism to gain and maintain political power, operating on the financial plane from his stronghold in Treadneedle Street [where the Bank of England was located]."

So Hitler was funded by the international conspiracy in the form of the Wall Street bankers and was also assisted in Germany's war effort by many U.S. manufacturers. In addition, Hitler had U.S. and British funds channeled to him, and had relations with people who were either actually in government, of at least had some ties to it.

An interesting tidbit lies in a popular song sung by the American soldiers, which poked fun at Hitler. One of the verses said. "We bring the world new order. Heil Hitler's New World Order!" (Hmmm ...?!)

Why would the Wall Street bankers and big industry want to aid Hitler? More importantly, why would the American and British governments want to help him? The same old reasons - profit and power! The bankers and industrialists would obviously profit greatly form another war... especially since the industrialists were *also the bankers* (being mostly Morgan, Warburg, Rockefeller and Rothschild interests). Furthermore, both the American and British governments were already controlled by the international banking conspirators...

The truth was that Roosevelt, a shrewd banker himself (who 'just happened' to have made a considerable amount of money in the 1920s by floating millions of dollars in worthless German bonds), and hungry for the power that the conspiracy could give him, wanted U.S. involvement in World War II from the very beginning... It was just a matter of making it publicly acceptable. A 1940 Gallup poll found 83 % of Americans were against participation in the European conflict, which meant that Roosevelt had to come up with a way to get us into the war.

Getting the U.S. involved in WWII became Roosevelt's primary goal. He assigned many people to work on the task. Finally, it was decided that it would be too difficult to get Germany to attack the U.S.; the only choice was to antagonize Japan into attacking us! Henry Stimpson, Roosevelt's War Secretary wrote: The question was how we should maneuver them [the Japanese] into the position of firing the first shot..." So some of Roosevelt's advisors on the war sent him a memorandum recommending a trade embargo against Japan, which he eventually enacted.

Roosevelt knew about the invasion of Pearl Harbor long before it happened! In *The Final Secret of Pearl Harbor,* Admiral Robert Theobald concludes that:

> 1) Roosevelt forced Japan to war and enticed them to initiate hostilities by holding the Pacific fleet in Hawaiian waters as an invitation to attack.

> 2) The plans to use Pearl Harbor as the bait started in June 1940 (18 months before the attack!).

> 3) War with Japan meant War with Germany (which is exactly what the conspiracy wanted).

> 4) Roosevelt, Marshall and Stark knew all about the impending attack on Pearl Harbor a full 21 hours before it happened!

As proof, Admiral Husband Kimmel, commander of the navel forces at Pearl Harbor, clearly places the blame for Pearl Harbor's unpreparedness on President Roosevelt. He wrote: "We were unready at Pearl Harbor, because President Roosevelt's plans required that no word be sent to alert the fleet in Hawaii."

The conspirators' plans were working perfectly. With their backing, Hitler had risen to power and World War 11 was going full tilt. And now, thanks to Roosevelt's treachery, the United States was also entering the war... But the treachery didn't stop there. The conspirators planned World War II not only to reap huge profits on all sides and force the United States into further debt and more socialism, but they also planned to use the war to seize greater control for their pet creation - the U.S.S.R.

Since the U.S.S.R. had been created by the conspirators (with considerable help from the U.S. politicians and bankers), it was not yet ready to fight an all-out war. To overcome this the U.S. government (under direction from the conspiracy) started shipping millions of American vehicles, ships and weapons for the Soviets to use - supposedly against Germany. Without this massive supply, it is doubtful they would have turned back the German army. You might say that the U.S. saved the country that later became its so-called greatest 'threat'.

One of the greatest war crimes in all of World War 11, which is completely left out of our history books, is the fact that Eastern Europe was purposely handed over to the Soviet Union on a silver platter! This was done when Churchill and Roosevelt, at the urging of the international banking conspiracy, made a secret pact with Stalin, *deliberately* delayed the plan of invasion of Europe from 1943 to 1944! This was to allow the Russians more time to gain control of a considerably larger area of Eastern Europe than they would have gotten had the U.S. and Great Britain attacked in 1943, as originally planned. The conspirators wanted to allow the Russians to gain more territory, because it moved them closer to their goal of world domination!

Attributing the decision to assist Russia in gaining more territory to Secretary of State George Marshall, Senator Joseph McCarthy made this comment: "We now come to what was without question the most significant decision of the war in Europe - the decision by Marshall to concentrate on France, and leave the whole of Eastern Europe to the Red Armies."

In fact, only the U.S.S.R. (read that as the conspirators) emerged as winners at the end of the war. Huge tracts of land were added to the Soviet empire, while Western Europe merely gained back what it lost to Hitler... And the U.S. was the big loser - just as the conspirators had wanted! Not only did the United States loose thousands of young lives needlessly, but the American people were saddled with paying off the war debts from all the countries involved, and were further stuck with paying for the rebuilding not only of Western Europe, Germany, and Russia, but Japan as well!!

U.S. General Albert C. Wedemeyer explained that:

"Stalin was intent on creating favorable conditions for the realization of Communist aims throughout the Balkans and Western Europe. We insured the emergence of a more hostile, menacing predatory power than Nazi Germany, one which has enslaved more people than we liberated."

Another wartime atrocity occurred in February of 1945 when Roosevelt met with Stalin at the Yalta conference, where it was agreed that all the Russian refugees that had come west would be returned to the U.S.S.R. This was termed by the U.S. troops as 'Operation Keelhaul.' Many thousands of Russian refugees preferred suicide rather than go back to Stalin, and many more thousands were murdered upon return! In total about 2 million refugees were rounded up by reluctant American and British troops and returned to the Soviet Union.

After the war, the negotiations and treaties saw the Allies make more and more concessions to the Soviets. The Soviets got so much more out of the negotiations that James Forrestal, America's first Secretary of Defense said: "These men are neither incompetent nor stupid. They are crafty and brilliant. Consistency has never been a mark of stupidity. If they were merely stupid, they would occasionally make a mistake in our favor."

Forrestal was obviously considered by the conspirators to be dangerous because he threatened their exposure. So he was later sent to Bethesda Navel Hospital where he died, supposedly from "falling" out of a window in an attempt to hang himself... but it was really murder! Indeed, the coroners report never even used the word "suicide."

Internationally known poet Ezra Pound also realized what the conspirators were up to, and exposed them on a national radio broadcast. Just before his imprisonment by the U.S. government as a 'political prisoner' (without a specific charge or trial), he said of his exposure of the conspirators: "I reckon my last talk was the most courageous I have ever given. I was playing with fire. I was openly talking about how the war may be prolonged by fellows who were scared that the war might stop. I mean they were scared right out of their little grey panties, for fear economic equity might set in as soon as the guns stop shooting or shortly thereafter."

Pound was labeled 'mentally ill,' and moved to St. Elizabeth's Psychiatric Hospital. Since the government is not required to hold a trial for anyone deemed 'mentally ill,' Pound never got one. This was all after Pound had played a major role in developing such poets and writers as E.E. Cummings, Robert Frost, T.S. Elliot, and Ernest Hemmingway, among others, and had become well known in his own right. He obviously posed a threat to 'the powers that be,' so they had him locked up!

Soon after the end of the war, Senator Joseph McCarthy accused many people in government of being Communists. He was, of course, entirely correct. 'Me government itself later substantiated what McCarthy had been saying when, on July 30th, 1953, it released a report entitled "interlocking Subversion in Government Departments", which was written by the Senate International Security Subcommittee- It read: "The Soviet international organization has carried on a successful and important penetration of the United States Government, and this penetration has not been fully exposed. This penetration has extended from the lower ranks to top-level policy and operating positions in our government. Despite the fact that the Federal Bureau of Investigation and other security agencies had reported extensive information about this Communist penetration, little was done by the Executive branch to interrupt the Soviet operatives in their ascent within our government. "

So things were getting much worse. Not only did the conspiracy have control of Roosevelt and much of Congress through the Council on Foreign Relations (CFR), but they had also gained control over most of the agencies of the U.S. government.

The final agreements of the war saw the creation of the Marshall Plan, which was overseen by the Economic Cooperation Administration (ECA). All of the aid channeled to Europe through the ECA was linked to purchases of particular American goods and services. Thus, the Marshall Plan subsidized some U.S. businesses (those already owned or controlled by the conspirators) at the expense of the taxpayer. Although the Marshall Plan was more realistic in its ability to maintain long-term peace that was the Treaty of Versailles, it was not at all a beneficial plan as far as America was concerned. It guaranteed that the American taxpayers would rebuild war-torn Europe and Japan - and even Russia - while the bankers collected hefty profits on the skyrocketing American debt, the interest on countless loans, and huge upswings in their business interests. In other words, the Marshall plan did exactly what the international banking conspiracy wanted: to further finance them - very handsomely (at America's expense) - after the war ended!

In summary, World War 11 was set up by the conspirators through the grossly unfair Treaty of Versailles (at the end of Word War 1), which completely destroyed the German economy, leading to the rise of Hitler to power. If the conspirators had not funded and supplied Hitler, the war (if it would have occurred at all) would have been relatively small and insignificant. Since the American people were largely opposed to involvement, Roosevelt (a banker himself) secretly plotted to get the U.S. into the war by antagonizing the Japanese, and enticed them to attack by sacrificing Pearl Harbor and thousands of lives. 'Men the conspirators (through secret agreements between Churchill, Roosevelt and Stalin), allowed the Soviets to grab as much territory as possible from Eastern Europe both during and after the war, and also allowed them to slaughter millions of returning refugees. Finally, the Marshall Plan continued to subsidize banking and big industry at the expense of American taxpayers after the war was over...

Indeed, it would seem that World War 11 had gone very well for the conspirators, advancing their ultimate goal of establishing the New World Order even better than they had hoped. But there was still much work to be done...

The United Nations

"Good intentions will always be pleaded for every assumption of power... It is hardly too strong to say that the Constitution was made to guard the people against the dangers of good intentions. There are men in all ages who mean to govern well, but they mean to govern. They promise to be good masters, but they mean to be masters."- Daniel Webster

During World War II, on January lst, 1942, the 25 nations at war against Germany and Japan signed a 'Declaration by the United Nations,' which pledged that any one nation involved would not sign a separate armistice or peace treaty. This was the beginning of the creation of the current United Nations. Once World War II was just a memory, the United Nations was to be formally made into an international organization, supposedly to help maintain the peace.

Following World War 11, the Council on Foreign Relations, acting through the State Department, established the United Nations on American soil, thus ensuring participation by the United States... John D. Rockefeller, one of the international banking conspirators, and an ardent supporter of the UN, donated $8.5 million (nearly $100 million in today's "dollars") to purchase the land and building for the UN headquarters in New York City.

The CFR, having persuaded America to join a limited form of world government, had achieved a major objective in its bid for domination of the world. Influencing public education and media, the CFR began to forge a favorable image of the United Nations as "promoting international peace, harmony and understanding" before. the American people, eventually intending to lead America step-by-step into a system of world government.

Its real purpose, however, ever since the official signing of the UN treaty in San Francisco on October 24th, 1945, has been to march us into a one-world totalitarian government. The CFR knew it would meet with stiff resistance from the American people if it tried to force world government upon America all at once. The immediate purpose of the UN, therefore, was to warm Americans up to the idea of global government. We were being 'conditioned' to accept the dictates of the international banking conspiracy through the United Nations' globalist leaders. The UN's record, the records of its members, and the things they have said only serve to support this fact... as in the following quotations:

"The UN is a true world organization. Actually, the creation of a world government, in any shape or form, depends not primarily upon the structure of an international organization, but upon the willingness of key countries to surrender certain sovereign rights." [Department of State Publication 3929]

John Foster Dulles, Eisenhower's first Secretary of State (not to mention accomplice to Hitler), wrote, "'Me United Nations represents not a final stage in the development of world order, but only a primitive stage. Therefore, its primary task is to create the conditions which will make possible a more highly developed organization."

Another significant piece of evidence pointing to a conspiracy to install a world government is the US government document *Freedom From War - State Dept Publication 7277,* which reads:

"1) The first stage would significantly reduce the capabilities of nations to wage war by reducing the armed forces of the nations;

2) The nuclear capabilities would be reduced by treaties;

3) UN 'peace keeping' powers would be strengthened. This third stage would have the nations retaining only those forces required for maintaining internal order, but the United States would provide manpower for the United Nations *Peace Force."* [An oxymoron - or contradiction of terms - if ever I heard one!]

This document was mysteriously taken out of print and circulation just a few years after it first came out. Could it be that it was just too close to what was *really* planned to happen?

Dr. J.B. Mathews, former chief investigator or the house committee on Un-American Activities said, "I challenge the illusion that the UN is an instrument of peace... It could not be less of a cruel hoax if it had been organized in Hell for the sole purpose of aiding an abetting the destruction of the Unit Stares. [From *The Fearful Master: a Second Look at the United Nations,* by G. Edward Griffin].

Joseph Stalin, one of the most despotic, tyrannical, and murderous dictators the world has ever seen, had this to say about the UN: "I attribute great importance to the UN, since it is a serious instrument for preservation of peace and international security."

Another top Communist Party member said, "Now, as to the United Nations. If you were, let's say, a building engineer, and someone were to show you a set of blueprints about a certain building, you would know from those blueprints how that building was going to look. Organizational 'blueprints' can be read the same way. I need not be a member of the United Nations Secretariat to know that the UN 'blueprint' is a Communist one. I was at the Moscow headquarters of the World Communist Party for nearly 3 years, and was also a leading party worker. I went to their colleges; I learned their pattern of operations, and if I see that pattern in effect anywhere, I can recognize it..."

The truth is that the UN is another brilliantly conceived, masterwork of deception - designed and implemented by the international banking conspiracy as a means of achieving their goal of world domination. They never intended the UN as a peace keeping organization. What they had in mind was a fancy and colossal Trojan horse, within the structure of which their smaller agencies could more effectively operate. And in that, they succeeded - even beyond their own expectations...

British espionage authority Chapman Pincher said, "Because of the protective cover they afford, all the major United Nations institutions have been heavily penetrated... Whole books have been published listing the abuse and manipulation of the United Nations by the Soviets and their international financier backers. The area most blatantly used for active measures and espionage is the main headquarters in New York."

One of the foremost plans of the United Nations is to take over the military operations of sovereign countries in order to form a 'New World Army.' The only problem with that objective was that it would have meant an end to wars that the conspiracy could instigate, orchestrate, manipulate, and finally reap profits from both sides of the conflict. They therefore decided to bide their time until such a move (toward creating a one-world army) would be not only feasible, but also practical. The problem was how could they move the world forward to such a place where nations would be willing to give up their standing armies?

They solved this problem in typical conspirators' fashion, by first creating another problem which would lead all nations into gladly surrendering their armies in the name of 'peace.' This was done by increasing the so-called Soviet 'threat,' to the point that - even though the United States and the Soviet Union were supposedly at a standoff in the famous 'cold war,' which lasted over 40 years -there was continual armed conflict spreading throughout the globe at an alarming pace... These conflicts were instigated by Soviet (read that as conspirator-paid) infiltrators, who purposely played upon the natural divisions of populations in order to incite war.

The result is that ever since the end of World War 11, in addition to the obvious Korean and Viet Nam wars, the earth has been in a constant state of turmoil over much of the globe. That these were not merely 'natural' conflicts between different demographic communities occupying the same area is proven by the fact that in nearly all of the areas of conflict, the populations had managed to co-exist peacefully for generations - or even centuries - before.

Finally, with the highly acclaimed 'collapse' of the Soviet Union (which was just another carefully orchestrated event to further the international banking conspirators' plans - as we *will* discuss in another section of this report), the world experienced a great sense of relief and even a sense of unity toward a bright, 'democratic' tomorrow - just as the conspirators had hoped. But instead of becoming more peaceful, the turbulence throughout the world had increased dramatically (with considerable help from the conspirators) since the collapse of the U.S.S.R.

Now, at last, they have us where they want us! The emphasis has been shifted from fighting between nations to internal conflict... Enter the 'benevolent' UN 'Peace Keeping' forces! These forces are not of any one nation, but of numerous nations - and always on foreign soil, to prevent any soldier from hesitating in firing on civilians. A Bosnian soldier might be reluctant to fire on Bosnian civilians, for example. Conversely, a Lithuanian soldier would not feel as much remorse in firing on American civilians as an American soldier would!

In its March 6th, 1992 article, "'Me New World Army'," the *New York Times* said, "For years the United Nations has been notable mostly for its vocal chords. That's changed. Nowadays the UN's muscle - its blue-helmeted soldiers - seem to be everywhere... Never before have so many UN troops been committed to so many costly and diverse missions."

The Los *Angeles Times of* September 8th, 1992, had an article by Norman Kempster, who wrote, "Creating a standing army under the control of the United

Nations Security Council would give the world organization a military punch never before had, and could convert it into a full-time international police department."

William Jasper, in his book, Global *Tyranny Step By Step,* asks, "In what social or economic spheres, if any, will the new world orderites *not* find a pretext for intervention? According to the new UN agenda, there are none. Among the 'new risks for stability' listed by the Secretary General are 'ecological damage' and 'disruption *of* family and community life." Other 'sources of conflict' include: 'unchecked population growth;' 'drugs and growing disparity between rich and poor;' 'poverty, disease, famine;' 'drought;' 'a porous ozone shield;' and about anything else you might imagine!"

Economist and author Dr. V. Orval Watts cited a true story in his book *The United Nations: Planned Tyranny.* It read: "At Fort MacArthur, California, and in other centers, considerable numbers of American military forces went into training in 1951 as 'Military Government Reserve Units.' The purpose of these reserve units is revealed from their practice maneuvers during the 2 years, 1951-1952.

The CFR soon realized, however, that regionalized world government would be impossible to achieve politically, because of the resistance to the idea from the citizens of each country... So they instead decided to divide the world into economic regions, such as the European Economic Community (formerly the Common Market), and the North American Free Trade Association (NAFTA), hoping to pave the way for later political unions based on the same geographical boundaries!

To accomplish this, several special-task organizations were established to oversee the creation of regional trade associations. The organization responsible for Europe's economic integration into the world government was the Bilderbergers, whose name was derived from the Bilderberg Hotel in Oosterbeck, Holland, where the group held their first meeting in 1945.

One hundred of the power elite from the member nations of NATO comprises the membership of the Bilderbergers. Its leaders are also interlocked with the CFR, making the Bilderbergers a sister organization with identical goals. Funded by several one-world foundations, including the Rockefeller and Ford foundations, the specific goal of the Bilderberg group is to regionalize Europe. This fact was first revealed by Giovanni Agnelli, head of Fiat (I always wondered if the Fiat company got its name from the fiat money we are all using?). Agnelli said, "European integration is our goal, and where the politicians have failed, we hope to succeed."

Former ambassador to West Germany, George McGhee, further revealed "the Treaty of Rome, which brought the Common Market into being, was nurtured at the Bilderberger meetings." The European Common Market would be the great giant step to crush the sovereignty of European nations.

Like the UN and CFR, the Bilderbergers' specific goal is the establishment of a world government. This was clearly explained by the first chairman of the group, Prince Bernhard of the Netherlands. "Here comes our greatest difficulty, for the governments of the free nations are elected by the people, and if they do something the people don't like, they are thrown out. It is difficult to reeducate the people who have been brought up on nationalism to the idea of relinquishing part of their sovereignty to a super national body. This is a tragedy."

The International Monetary Fund (IMF) / World Bank

In July 1944, a group of international financiers and politicians met in Bretton Woods, New Hampshire, to come up with a global economic recovery plan for the ravages of WWII, and to promote global economic cooperation. It was officially called, "The United Nations Monetary and Financial Conference," but is typically known as the Bretton Woods Conference. At this conference, two international economic organizations were created: The International Monetary Fund (IMF), and The World Bank.

The two chief drafters of the Bretton Woods agreement, John Maynard Keynes and Harry Dexter White, were dedicated socialists and followers of the Rothschilds. Keynes was the darling of the British Fabian Society, the gang of socialist conspirators who had taken over and wrecked Great Britain. White was a member of the Council on Foreign Relations and a dedicated Soviet agent, who had moved into various positions of importance in the U.S. Treasury Department, where he carefully laid out plans for a new monetary order. Such were the men who designed our current world monetary system!

Although the motives of the conference appeared noble at the surface, the true motives behind the conference were anything but. One result of the conference was to take the world off the discipline of gold, which would allow countries (read that as the international banks) to inflate their currencies freely, without any restraint, other than the exchange rate with other currencies.

The second result of the conference was to create the World Bank (which was essentially a Federal Reserve for the world), and the International Monetary Fund, which was supposed to be a means for recovering nations to borrow money reasonably - but actually was a way to extort infinite amounts of money from the member nations, to be used in any way the international banking conspiracy wanted.

Here's how it worked (and still does today!): The IMF "loaned" millions of dollars to "needy" countries in order to "develop" them. The countries, over time, are supposed to pay the IMF back. However, the vast majority of the time (nearly 100%!), these "backward" countries default on the loans. The supporting members of the UN and IMF [World Bank then pick up the tab (the major portion of which always falls to America to repay). This does two things for the international conspiracy: first, it gives them a 'legitimate' reason to extort more money from the supporting nations' citizens (mostly the United States), which helps them to reach their goal of lowering the living standards of the more affluent nations; and second, it allows the international conspirators to buy the support of these backward countries for a one-world dictatorship.

The IMF has become the final guarantor of the loans of the world. Most of these are to third world countries that will never be paid back. Unfortunately, the wealthy nations of the UN (particularly the U.S.) ultimately pay for these loans through subsidies to the IMF, which of course comes from taxes. A perfect example of this: in 1988 the World Bank loaned Poland successive amounts of money starting with $17.9 million. Three years later, when the Polish government could not pay the $3.8 billion debt it had accumulated, President Bush advocated "debt forgiveness" and cancelled 70% of the amount owed to the U.S. Taxpayers picked up the bill.

This policy is exactly what the global conspirators want. They want to drag the economies of the wealthy industrialized nations down, and to raise the economies of the poorer countries; to whatever degree they can, in order to facilitate a comfortable merging of all countries into a one-world government. In addition, this process increases their control immensely, because they have the power to subjugate the wealthy countries through taxes, regulations and economic control. This policy also gives them control over the poor countries because the conspirators have essentially 'bought' them.

After studying the World Bank for several years, James Bovard concluded in his report entitled "The World Bank vs. the World's Poor" the following: "The Bank exists largely to maximize the transfer of resources to Third World governments. And by so doing, the bank has greatly promoted the nationalization of Third World economies and has increased political and bureaucratic control over the lives of the poorest of the poor. Bank officials are now leading a rhetorical crusade in favor of the private sector. Yet every time the bank loudly praises the private sector, it silently damns its own record. More than any other international institution, the bank is responsible for the rush to socialism in the Third World - the rise of political power over the private sector - and the economic collapse of Africa."

An article by Warren T. Brookes in the *Boston Herald* of March 20th, 1986 states: "...the UN's International Monetary Fund and the post-World War 11 monetary system... has been working for almost half a century to create a centrally controlled economic system for the planet. The IMF has also regularly created sufficient turmoil to topple governments and steer nations into the type of government-directed economic planning it favors."

Renown British author, A.K. Chesterton, who attended the Bretton Woods conference, declared in his book, *The New Unhappy Lords:* "The final act of Bretton Woods, which gave birth to the World Bank and the International Monetary Fund... and many similar assemblies of hand-picked functionaries - were not incubated by hard-pressed governments engaged in waging war, but by a Supra-national Power which could afford to look ahead to the shaping of a post-war world that would serve its interests."

In 1987, Senator Jesse Helms stated: "It is no secret that the international bankers profiteer from sovereign state debt. The New York banks have found important profit centers in the lending to countries plunged into debt by socialist regimes. Under socialist regimes, countries go deeper and deeper into debt because socialism as an economic system does not work. International bankers are sophisticated enough to understand this phenomenon, and they are also sophisticated enough to profit from it... The New York banks find the profit from the interest on this sovereign debt to be critical to their balance sheets. Up until very recently, this has been an essentially riskless game for the banks, because the IMF and the World Bank have stood ready to bail the banks out with our taxpayers' money."

One of designers of the Bretton Woods agreement and a long-time conspiracy insider, John Maynard Keynes, wrote a book called *The Economic Consequences of Peace,* in which he writes: "Lenin is said to have declared that the best ways to destroy the Capitalist system was to debauch the currency. By a continuing process of inflation, governments can confiscate, secretly and unobserved, an important part of the wealth of their citizens. By this method, they not only confiscate, but they confiscate arbitrarily, and while the process impoverishes many, it actually enriches some.

"Lenin was certainly right. There is no subtler, no surer means of overturning the existing basis of society than to debauch the currency. The process engages all the hidden forces of economic law on the side of the destructors, and does it in a manner not one man in a million is able to diagnose."

Economist Dan Smoot observed in 1979: "White's Bretton Woods Conference set policies which our government has followed, without deviation, under all Presidents, since the end of World War 11. These policies were intended to accomplish four major objectives:

> 1) Strip the United States of its monetary gold reserve by giving gold to other nations.

2) Build the industrial capacity of other nations, at our expense, to eliminate American productive superiority.

3) Take world markets - and much of the American domestic market - away from American producers to stop American domination of world trade.

4) Entwine American affairs with those of other nations until the United States could not have an independent policy, but would become an interdependent link in a worldwide socialist chain."

Henry Hazlitt wrote of Bretton Woods: "...[Regarding] the consequences of the decisions made by the representatives of the 45 nations at Bretton Woods... These decisions, and the institutions set up to carry them out, have led us to the present world monetary chaos. For the first time in history, every nation is on an inconvertible paper money basis (thanks to the international banking conspiracy). As a result, every nation is inflating [its currency], some at an appalling rate. This has brought economic disruption, chronic unemployment, and anxiety, destitution, and despair to untold millions of families... The world cannot get back to economic sanity until the IMF is abolished... We will not stop the growth of world inflation and world socialism until the institutions and policies adopted to promote them have been abolished."

The North American Treaty Organization (NATO) was created in 1949, not long after the UN and IMF/World Bank. It was supposedly created as an anti-communist alliance - but according to the Council on Foreign Relations, NATO's purpose was much more sinister, as the April, 1948 issue of the CFR's publication, *Foreign Affairs,* explains: "A regional organization of nations [such as NATO], formed to operate within the framework of the United Nations, can only strengthen that organization [the UN]." The article went on to indicate that NATO could very well serve as the military of a UN world government, with the World Bank as the global government's [the UN's] means of finance.

More recently, on April 2nd, 1992, the UN passed the United Nations International Covenant on Civil and Political Rights. There they go again, granting "Rights" to the 'common, unwashed masses', as if they were masters and the rest of us mere slaves... for that is exactly how they look at themselves - and don't ever forget the real truth as stated in our Declaration of Independence: "All men [and women - or all people] are created equal, and are endowed by their Creator with certain unalienable rights." In other words, we are given our rights by God - not some two-bit little bureaucrats and dictators!

Before the vote on the Covenant, Senator Jesse Helms said of it: "Now this Senator and every other Member of Congress has taken an oath of office to protect and defend the Constitution of the United States. And that means we should be fully committed to the rights of the individual, which are enshrined in our Constitution. And we should be committed to the protection of these individual rights. We cannot keep that commitment if we agree to the terms of this covenant!" Helms continued by saying that "The covenant calls into question the right of freedom of speech, and freedom of the press, and just punishments - they are clearly constitutional -and even the Federal/State structure of our legal system. Now any agreement that undercuts these rights is an attack on human rights, not a safeguarding of human rights. This covenant, in sum, is a step backwards into authoritarianism..."

Some excepts from the Covenant include:

*Article 10 - "The right to leave any country shall be subject only to such restrictions as are prescribed by law." (What restrictions? Prescribed by whom? Under what law?')

* Article 13 - "The child shall have the right to freedom of expression; freedom to seek, receive and impart

information and ideas of all kinds, regardless of frontiers, either orally, in writing or in print, in the form of art, or through any other media of the child's choice." This is a blatant step toward eliminating family - especially parental - influence over children. The State would be in control of what the children see or hear - or learn... So that the children can be more easily indoctrinated with the views of the State. Parents will be hauled before a world court if they "infringe" on the child's "right" to watch or read whatever garbage, propaganda, doctrine, or even filth the State has already "approved" as "educational" for children... including pornography or - even worse - "turn your parents in as criminals if they speak out against the State" Oust like Hitler did!). There is no mention of parents' rights!

* Article 14 - "Everybody shall be entitled to a fair and public hearing..." but then goes on to say, "The press and the public may be excluded from all or part of a trial for reasons of morals, public order..." (How can you have a 'public' hearing if the press and the public are excluded?

* Article 18 - "Everyone shall have the right to freedom of thought [Gee, Thanks!], conscience, and religion..." but then goes on to say, "Freedom to manifest one's religion or beliefs may be subject only to such limitations as are prescribed by law and are necessary." (Prescribed by whom? For what law? And 'necessary' by whose definition?)

* Article 28 - Recognizes the "right of the child to education," and would "make primary education compulsory and available to all." It also states that education must teach, "The principles enshrined in the Charter of the United Nations." (Yikes! Talk about "Big Brother"! ...)

"Me rest of the document continues like that. It grants a "right" or "freedom", and then creates vague conditions or exceptions, so that the "right" or "freedom" can be arbitrarily taken away. The document should read, "We 'give' you these rights [which aren't theirs to give in the first place!], unless or until we feel like taking them away." In essence, this Covenant of the "benevolent" UN is a hollow, deceitful, and thinly disguised, irreversible contract into slavery!

The frightening fact is that already 134 countries have signed in agreement to this fiendish and despotic 'Covenant' (with whom - Satan himself?)... The United States has not signed in agreement yet - but it is being 'considered'!

By the way, the United States (read that as the American taxpayers) pays a full 25% of all the expenses of the United Nations!! If we are to preserve our freedom and God-given rights for future generations and ourselves... if there is to be a United States of America in the future... we must withdraw America completely from the United Nations *IMMEDIATELY!* and withdraw all of our monetary support!

The Korean War and the Vietnam War

The Korean and Vietnam wars have a lot in common. Both were aftermaths of WWII, resulting from instigation and manipulation by the international banking conspiracy for their usual goals of reaping profits on both sides, expanding their control over the globe through socialism, and pushing the U.S. closer to bankruptcy. Both wars could have been easily avoided (were it not for instigation by the conspirators). Both wars were lost by the U.S. (on purpose!). Both wars were I non-wars' (undeclared). And most importantly, both wars were under the auspices and control of the UN.

The only reason the U.S. got involved with both the Korean and Vietnam wars was to validate NATO and make it acceptable for U.S. troops to fight under UN command.

In addition, the U.S. (actually the UN) never intended to win either war. That would have caused the Communists, whom the conspirators supported, to lose territory. To prevent success in these wars, ridiculous rules of engagement were established, and allied intelligence information was often passed on to the communists. For example, during the Korean War, according to Douglas MacArthur's *Reminiscences, "[U.S.* General Walton Walker] continually complained that his operations were known to the enemy in advance through sources in Washington."

MacArthur went on to quote General Lin Piao as saying, "I would never have made the attack and risked my men... if I had not been assured that Washington would restrain General MacArthur from taking adequate retaliatory measures against my lines of supply and communications."

Further proof that the war was "rigged" and the U.S. wasn't allowed to win, comes from George Straterneyer, a general in the Air Force during the Korean War, who said, "We had sufficient air, bombardment, fighters, reconnaissance, so that I could have taken out all of those supplies, those airdromes on the other side of the Yalu; I could have bombarded the devils between there and Mukden, stopped the railroad operating, and the people of China who were fighting could not have been supplied. But we weren't permitted to do it. As a result, a lot of American blood was spilled over there in Korea."

Meanwhile, the international conspiracy was continuing to strengthen its position in the U.S. government. Norman Thomas, president of the Socialist Party in the U.S. at this time described their progress under the presidency of Eisenhower, saying, "The United States is making greater strides towards Socialism under Eisenhower than even under Roosevelt. "

One of the most significant of these "strides towards Socialism" was the defeat of the Bricker Amendment, which stipulated that no treaty signed by the U.S. could override the Constitution or infringe on the rights guaranteed Americans. Had this bill passed, it would have been a tremendous blow to the global conspirators... Stephen Ambrose, in his biography of Eisenhower said, "Eisenhower used all his persuasive powers - in stag dinners, at meetings, in private, in correspondence, even on the golf course - to kill the Bricker Amendment." So the bill was killed. The question remains, however: What harm could this bill have done to anyone besides someone attempting to infringe upon or circumvent the Constitution? By the way, most Americans were never even aware of the bill's existence at the time!

Although Eisenhower was involved with the conspirators to some degree, he felt obliged to issue the following warning to all Americans in his farewell address of January 17th, 1961:

"In the councils of government, we must guard against the acquisition of unwarranted influence, whether sought or unsought, by the military-industrial complex. The potential for the disastrous rise of misplaced power exists and will persist. We must never let the weight of this combination endanger our liberties or democratic processes. We should take nothing for granted. Only an alert and knowledgeable citizenry can compel the proper meshing of the huge industrial and military machinery of defense with our peaceful methods and goals, so that security and liberty may prosper together."

The conspirators never intended the United States to win in Vietnam, either. As proof, take a look at the "rules of engagement" for the U.S. military in Vietnam, as passed down to the executive branch of the U.S. government from the conspirators through the CFR:

- The Air Force was repeatedly refused permission to bomb those targets that were deemed most strategic.

- U.S. troops were given a general order not to fire upon Viet Cong until fired upon.

- Vehicles more than 200 yards off the Ho Chi Minh Trail could not be bombed.

- Surface to air missile sights could not be bombed while under construction, only after they were operational.

- Enemy forces could not be pursued if they crossed into Laos or Cambodia.

Another unbelievable aspect of the Vietnam War was that the U.S. (read that as 'the conspiracy') was really supplying *both* sides! The United States was sending massive amounts of supplies to the USSR, which in turn sent those same supplies straight to North Vietnam!

Still further proof that the conspirators were stacking the deck against America comes from the front line, where American boys were purposely issued the inferior M-16 rifle, which - because its very design was flawed - was almost worse than having no weapon at all! The June, 1981 issue of *The Atlantic Monthly* relates the following observations made by an American soldier on the front lines in Vietnam:

"Our M- l6s aren't worth much... Out of 40 rounds I've fired, my rifle jammed about 10 times ... These rifles are getting a lot, of guys killed because they jam so easily... The weapon has failed us at crucial moments ... as many as 50% of the rifles fail to work... During this fight I lost some of my best buddies. I personally checked their weapons. Close to 70% had a round stuck in the chamber, and take my word for it - it was not their fault!"

All of this was obviously covered up by the government. In 197 1, Louisiana Congressman John Rarick pointed this out:

"The My Lai massacre, the sentencing of Lt. Calley to life imprisonment, 'The Selling of the Pentagon,' and the so-called 'Pentagon Papers', are leading examples of attempts to shift all the blame to the military in the eyes of the people. But no one identifies the Council on Foreign Relations (the CFR) - a group of some 1400 "Americans" (they aren't worthy of that name), which includes as members almost every top level decision and policy maker in the Vietnam War.

"CBS tells the people that it wants them to know what is going on, and who is to blame. Why doesn't CBS tell the American people about the CFR, and let the people decide whom to blame for the Vietnam fiasco: the planners and top decision makers of a closely knit, financial control..."

It is important to note that by this time, the conspiracy had complete control of the U.S. government... For example, President Lyndon Johnson even stated, "We are going to take all the money *we think is unnecessarily being spent* [emphasis added), and take it from the 'haves' and give it to the 'have-nots' that need it so much. "(!!!) This was the basis for his "Great Society" program... which is no different than the Communist Manifesto's statement: "From each according to his ability, to each according to his need!

WOW! All I can say is:

"Hey, LBJ! How about all those 'haves' - the international banking conspiracy - who stole outright practically all the property, wealth, gold, and silver (not to mention the freedom, rights, privacy, and - in far too many cases the very lives) of the citizens of this once great nation? How about making *771EM* give all 'their' money - stolen from the American citizens (which we KNOW is unnecessarily being spent), and giving it back to its rightful owners, the American people, who now (thanks to 'them'), are <u>ALL</u> 'have nots!"

In summary, neither the Korean nor the Vietnam wars were fought with the intention of winning. They were fought to: suck more money out of America and place it in the hands of the conspiracy created communists; to create more enormous profits from both sides for the bankers; to insure the further acquisition of territory for the communists/conspirators; to push America even further into Socialism; to lend credibility to NATO; and to establish a precedent of the U.S. military fighting under UN authority. Furthermore, the one-world conspirators had effectively gained control of the majority of the U.S. government as one more step in their plan of establishing a world dictatorship.

The Report From Iron Mountain

"War is Peace. ' - George Orwell

The "Report From Iron Mountain" was a confidential document prepared by nine members of the U.S. department of Defense while it was headed by Robert McNamara, in 1966. It was produced by the Hudson Institute which is located at the base of Iron Mountain in New York - hence the name. The primary purpose of this report was to find ways to perpetuate government and to subjugate the masses. The most important goal of the report, however, was to study the function of war, its uses and effects on society, and to come up with alternatives to war as a means of controlling society.

The text of the report clearly reveals the almost unbelievably shocking and disgusting total arrogance of the general mentality of the conspirators - their complete disregard and in fact disdain for the rest of the population, whom they consider to be no more than their chattel! It exposes the conspirators' typical supremacist attitude, in which the masses don't have the intelligence to be able to run their own lives, and therefore can - and should be used like mere pawns in a chess game, to help insure the positions of power and control which rightfully belong to the conspirators as more supremely intelligent and capable. The most blatant proof of their utter snobbery is demonstrated clearly in this report by their total disregard of the suffering and loss of human life caused by war - which the conspirators deem "necessary" in order to maintain and increase their control over the rest of us - 'for the good of humanity.'... This unconscionable and nauseating mentality is best expressed in their own words... For that reason, much of this section will be dedicated to directly quoting the report itself. If you are able to read the following paragraphs without getting sick to your stomach, then you are doing much better than I did!

The following excepts are direct quotes form *The Report from Iron Mountain on the Possibility and Desirability of Peace:*

"War has provided both ancient and modern society with a debatable system for stabilizing and controlling national economies. No alternate method of control has yet been tested in a complex modem economy that has shown it is remotely comparable in scope of effectiveness. War fills certain functions essential to the stability of our society, until other ways of filling them are developed, the war system must be maintained and improved in effectiveness

"War... is the principle organizing force in most societies. The possibility of war provides the sense of external necessity without which no government can long remain in power.

"Allegiance requires a cause, and a cause requires an enemy. This much is obvious. The critical point is that the enemy that defines the cause must seem genuinely formidable. Roughly speaking, the presumed power of the 'enemy' sufficient to warrant an individual sense of allegiance to a power must be one of unprecedented magnitude and frightfulness.

"'Me existence of an accepted external menace, then, is essential to social cohesiveness, as well as to the acceptance of political authority. The menace must be believable, it must be of a magnitude consistent with the complexity of the society threatened, and it must appear, at least, to affect the entire society.

"The war system not only has been essential to the existence of nations an independent political entities, but has been equally indispensable to their stable political structure. Without it, no government has ever been able to obtain acquiescence in its 'legitimacy,' or right to rule its society. The historical record reveals one instance after another where the failure of a regime to maintain the credibility of a war threat led to its dissolution, by the forces of private interest, of reactions to social injustice, or of other disintegrative elements. The organization of society for the possibility of war is its principal political stabilizer... It has enabled societies to maintain necessary class distinctions, and-it has insured the subordination of the citizens to the state by virtue of the residual war powers inherent in the concept of nationhood."

The report goes on to say that this 'war system' could now be obsolete, because a world government may now be possible. For this to occur, however, the global power would have to come up with alternative. Reasons (threats and/or problems) with which to organize society and subjugate the people.

As it explains:

"A viable substitute for war as a social system cannot be a mere symbolic charade. It must involve real risk of real personal destruction and on a scale consistent with the size and complexity of modem social systems. Unless it provides a believable life-and-death threat, it will not serve the socially organizing function of war.

"Credibility, in fact, lies at the heart of the problem of developing a political substitute for war... It may be that the gross pollution of the environment can eventually replace the possibility of mass destruction by nuclear weapons, as the principle apparent threat to the survival of the species. Poisoning of the air, and of the main sources of food and water supply is already well advanced, and at first glance would seem promising in this respect. [!!!] It [environmental poisoning] constitutes a threat that can be dealt with only through social organizations and political power. But from present indications, it will be one to one and one-half generations before environmental pollution, however severe, will be sufficiently menacing, on a global scale, to offer a possible basis for a solution." [Bear in mind that this report was made about 30 years ago - or approximately one and one-half generations!)

The *Report From Iron Mountain* was to come up with alternatives to war as a means of controlling society. The producers of this report concluded that nothing was as effective as war, but there were other promising possibilities...

First, the replacement(s) for war must meet the following requirements: 1) It must be economically wasteful. (!! Why am I not surprised?) 2) It must operate outside the normal supply-demand system. 3) It must represent a threat of great magnitude. 4) It must provide a logical excuse for compulsory service to the government.

Next, these are some of the substitutes for war the writers of the Report came up with:

1) Complete government health care for all.

2) A guaranteed annual income.

3) A series of giant space research programs aimed at unreachable targets.

4) The specter of gross pollution as a threat to the survival of the species.

5) The re-introduction of slavery through some form of compulsory military service.

6) A universal requirement that procreation be limited to the products of artificial insemination.

7) A massive, all I -encompassing social welfare program.

Finally, the report concluded that: "no serious quantified studies have ever been conducted to determine... the minimum levels of population destruction [!] necessary to maintain war-threat credibility under varying political conditions;" and 11 optimal cyclical frequency of 'shooting' wars under varying circumstances of historical relationships." Essentially what this means is that no one knows how many people should be killed, and how frequently they should be killed, in order to credibly maintain the threat of war!! (What kind of cold-blooded monsters are we dealing with here, anyway?)

When the *Report From Iron Mountain* was first leaked to the press, the U.S. government claimed it was a hoax, which has caused many people to doubt its credibility. This, of course, is exactly what the conspirators wanted... because, as we have already learned, their first weapon is always concealment and deception. Since that time, however, many people involved in the creation of the report have come forward and admitted not only the existence of the report itself, but also their involvement in its production. Among those is well-known historian John Kenneth Galbraith of Harvard University, who said, "As I would put my personal repute behind the authenticity of this document, so would I testify to the validity of its conclusions. "

Most of the suggestions and conclusions mentioned above have already either come to pass, or are in their final planning stages... The writers of the *Report,* however, decided that the best alternative to war was the environmental pollution model. Recent history bears this out with the advent of all kinds of environmental "crises" arising:

State of the World 1991, the annual report issued by the globalist World Watch Institute, says: "The battle to save the planet will replace the battle over ideology as the organizing theme of the new world order."

"Me *Washington Post* of November 12th, 1989, had an article entitled "There Is No Time For Talk of German Reunification" by George Kennon (CFR member) which said, "We must prepare for... an age where the great enemy is not the Soviet Union, but the rapid deterioration of our planet as a supporting structure for civilized life."

Norman Cousins (CFR member) said, "Humanity needs a world order. The fully sovereign nation is incapable of dealing with the poisoning of the environment... 'Me management of the planet, therefore - whether we are talking about the need to prevent war or the need to prevent ultimate damage to the conditions of life - requires world government. "

The council of the Club of Rome (one of the better-known organizations of the conspiracy) said in their report, *The First Global Revolution,* "In searching for a new enemy to unite us, we came up with the idea that pollution, the threat of global warming, water shortages, famine and the like would fit the bill... All of these dangers are caused by human intervention [in most cases, by the conspirators themselves from behind the scenes!]... The real enemy, then, is humanity itself." (That is at least partially correct, in that the conspirators all claim to be human - although their actions and agenda would seem to prove otherwise!)

The Club of Rome

"The winds of change have begun to blow"
- Aurelio Peccei

Founded in April, 1968, when leaders from ten different countries gathered in Rome at the urging of the international banking conspiracy through private invitation from Aurelio Peccei (an Italian industrialist associated with Fiat automobiles and the Olivetti company), the Club of Rome claims to have the solutions for world peace and prosperity. These solutions, however, always promote the concept of one-world government at the expense of personal freedom and national sovereignty.

Drawing a large number of its members from the CFR, the Club of Rome (COR) claims to be an "informal" organization of less than 100 scientists, educators, economists humanists, industrialists, and international l civil servants', including members of the Rockefeller family. 25 CFR members belong to the American Association for the Club of Rome.

The international banking conspiracy charged the Club of Rome with the task of administrating the regionalization and unification of the entire world into 10 economic and political "kingdoms," of which the European Common Market (now referred to as "the European Economic Community"), and NAFTA are only the beginning! Indeed, most of the directives for the planning of one-world government have their origins with the Club of Rome!

It is interesting to note that at this time - during the Nixon administration - the United States was divided into 10 federal sub-regions, for "emergency management" (in case of an insurrection by the American citizens)... The public was told that it was for "decentralization of the Executive Branch." (Yeah, sure!)... These regions are most evident today in our court system (which has 10 federal "districts"); the military - supposedly for purposes of deployment - but more accurately for purposes of 1) invasion by UN "peace keeping" forces consisting of foreign troops on our soil to keep us under control), and 2) internment into the already existing and operational "concentration camps," which have been established at numerous military bases in the U.S. which were supposedly "closed" because we no longer face the conspiracy-contrived "Soviet threat"; the postal service (if you want to know which of the 10 "districts" you live in, just check out the first number - 0 through 9 - of your Zip code).

In reality, this artificial division of the United States into 10 regions was sort of a "test run" for the ultimate division of the entire world! No discussion of the primary task of the Club of Rome would be complete without recognizing that the in the last book of the Bible - called either the "Revelations" or the "Apocalypse" - there exists the prediction that before the final conflict (which seems to be drawing closer by the minute!), the world would be -divided into "ten kingdoms. "

The Club of Rome revealed its intentions (and thus the intentions of the international banking conspiracy) in its 1974 book (which was intended for the public), entitled *Mankind at the Turning Point:* "The solutions of these [conspiracy-contrived] crises (economic control, food shortages, environmental, etc.) can be developed only in a global context, with full and explicit recognition of the emerging world system, and on a long-term basis. This would necessitate, among other changes, a new world economic order and a global resources allocation system. A world consciousness must be developed through which every individual realizes his role as a member of the world community. It must become part of the consciousness of every individual that the basis of human cooperation (and hence survival) lies in moving from the national to the global level."

The Trilateral Commission

"The standard of living of the average American has to decline... I don't think you can escape that.
- Paul Volcker

Congressional leaders and citizens' action groups began to expose the Council on Foreign Relations during the 1950s and 60s. By the late 1960s and early 70s, the sinister plot of the CFR was reaching the American people, despite the lack of media coverage. Americans, for the first time, became aware that major portions of American industry were dominated and controlled by only a few organizations.

The international banking conspiracy realized they had to do something before they lost their 50-year advantage, so they devised plans to funnel American and European money to Japanese industrialists and Arab oil emirates with instructions to purchase American real estate and American companies. By doing so, the conspirators gained complete control of American industry and, if anything went wrong with the economy or their plans, they had two perfect scapegoats to present to the American public (the Japanese and the Arabs).

Arab leaders, ever unable to live in harmony, suddenly became dearest friends overnight and imposed the oil embargo of 1973. Arab oil was being discovered, drilled and processed by American and European cartels, which were owned by members of the international banking conspiracy. The emirates only had to sit back and let their masters make them wealthy! The truth is that the oil emirates owe most of their wealth to the conspirators (especially the Rockefellers and Rothschilds).

A large portion of the oil wealth was immediately laundered back to the Chase Manhattan Bank, and some of the Arab sheiks actually became vice-presidents of the banks. Large amounts of the money were invested into American industry and real estate.

The great "oil crisis" (created entirely by the conspiracy!) turned Japan into an industrial giant. The Japanese auto manufacturers had compact cars - and Americans, forced to cut back energy consumption as a result of the contrived oil crisis, rushed to purchase Japan's inexpensive, fuel-efficient automobiles. Japanese imports were protected under our liberal "free-trade" laws. At the same time, American auto manufacturers sank into a recession from which they will never fully recover.

Japanese industrialists invested heavily in other Japanese industries, and America was soon inundated with inexpensive imports ranging from consumer electronics to industrial robots. Like the Arab money, much of their profits were used to purchase real estate in America and throughout the rest of the world (as they were instructed by the conspiracy to do)!

The result was that the "oil crisis" served to advance the New World Order faster than even inside planners could have dreamed. By working with Japanese and Arab co-conspirators, the globalists began to promote their agenda for world domination with little suspicion. The redistribution of the wealth of the world is being used to advance a new concept of "global economic interdependence," laying the groundwork for the one world government. To administer and address these goals, the Trilateral Commission was created.

The Trilateral Commission (so named for the "3 sides" - the United States, Europe, and Japan) was founded by David Rockefeller in 1972, and had its first meeting on July 24th and 25th of that year. The purpose of this organization according to the Trilateralists, is "close Trilateral cooperation in keeping the peace, in managing the world economy [!!], in fostering economic re-development and alleviating world poverty, will improve the chances of smooth and peaceful evolution of the global system." All that from a group who has not been elected, is of no country, and is made of bankers, big business men, and bought-and-paid-for politicians!"

The real purpose of the Trilaterals is far from being anything so beneficial. As Senator Barry Goldwater observed in his insightful *With No Apologies:* "In my view, the Trilateral Commission represents a skillful coordinated effort to seize control and consolidate the four centers of power: political, monetary, intellectual, and ecclesiastical... What the Trilateralists, truly intend is the creation of a worldwide economic power superior to the political governments of the nation-states involved... As managers and creators of the system, they will rule the future."

The true purpose behind the Trilaterals is further stated by John Knowles, president of the Rockefeller Foundation in 1975: "The web ['noose' would be a better word!] of interdependence is tightening. We are one world, and there will be but one future - for better or for worse - for us all."

The fact is, the Trilateral Commission promotes one world government by encouraging economic interdependence among the superpowers, steering the economies of member nations into a position where they would be forever completely enmeshed... It has become a carbon copy of the Council on Foreign Relations, having many of the same members, expressing the same philosophies, and funded by the same foundations (most notably Rockefeller and Carnegie). All eight American representatives to the founding meeting were members of the CFR.

Richard Gardener, top adviser to President Jimmy Carter, and member of the Trilaterals, explained the method of achieving world government: "...the 'house of world order' will have to be built from the bottom up rather than from the top down... An end run around national sovereignty, eroding it piece by piece, will accomplish far more than did the old fashioned frontal assaults."

This would seem to be supported by the fact that David Rockefeller has met with 27 heads of state, including Russia and China... done, no doubt, with the intention of explaining the conspiracy's plan, and insuring the rulers that they will have a place in the "New World Order."

The Rockefeller Foundation is one of the driving forces behind the Trilateral Commission. Gary Allen, a researcher of Rockefeller history, has been "unable to find. A single project in the history of the Rockefeller foundations which promotes free-enterprise."... The- October l2th, 1977 issue of the *Review of the News,* supports this view: "International Communism of the Moscow order has many features in common with David Rockefeller's Trilateral Commission - such as undermining the national sovereignty of the United States. It is for this reason that one finds so many known Marxists supporting the goals of the new world economic order sought by the Trilateral Commission.

Another founding member and later director of the Trilateral Commission was Zbigniew Brzezinski. He wrote a book in 1970 called *Between Two Ages,* in which he hopes for a new monetary system to replace the dollar; and a reduced living standard to achieve it. He goes on to say, "In the economic-technological field, some international cooperation has already been achieved, but further progress-will require greater American sacrifices. More intensive efforts to shape a new world monetary structure will have to be undertaken, with some consequent risk to the present relatively favorable American position."

He went on to say, "At the same time, the capacity to assert social and political control over the individual will vastly increase. It will soon be possible to assert almost continuous control over every citizen [!], and to maintain up-to-date files, containing even the most personal details about health and personal behavior of every citizen [!!], in addition to the more customary data.

"These files will be subject to instantaneous retrieval by the authorities. Power will gravitate into the hands of those who control information." [Zbigniew Brzezinski)

To corroborate this "Big Brother" line of thinking, I offer this quote from Edward Bernays, a psychologist and an

associate of the conspiracy inner circle, who wrote a book entitled *Propaganda,* in which he said: "We - e are governed,

our minds are molded, our tastes formed, our ideas suggested, largely by men we have never heard of. Whatever attitude

one chooses to take toward this condition, it remains a fact that in almost every act of our daily lives, whether in the

sphere of politics or business, our social conduct or our ethical thinking, we are dominated by a relatively small number

of persons... who understand the mental processes and social patterns of the masses. It is they who pull the wires which

control the public mind, and who harness old social forces and contrive new ways to bind and guide the world." It is a matter of public record that Bernays later held a top position in CBS.

As Dr. John Coleman, an international espionage agent (specializing in the conspiracy) explains: "There is not one single aspect of life in America that is not watched over, steered in the 'right' direction, manipulated, and controlled by the invisible government ... " [Conspirators' *Hierarchy,* John Coleman]

Zbigniew Brzezinski continues: "...Our existing institutions will be supplanted by pre-crisis management institutions, the task of which will be to identify - in advance - likely social crises, and to develop programs to cope with them. This will encourage tendencies through the next several decades toward a technetronic era - a dictatorship - leaving even less room for political procedures as we know them."

... By the way, Zbigniew Brzezinski was also President Carter's national security adviser!

President Carter was also heavily involved with the formation of the Trilateral Commission. *The Washington Post* of January 16th, 1977, revealed this about President Jimmy Carter: "If you like conspiracy theories about secret plots to take over the world, you are going to love the administration of President-elect Jimmy Carter! At last count, 13 Trilaterals had gone into top positions in the administration. This is extraordinary when you consider that the Trilateral Commission has only about 65 American members."

Senator Barry Goldwater explained Carter's role in the Trilaterals: "David Rockefeller and Zbigniew Brzezinski found Jinuny Carter to be their ideal candidate. They helped him win the nomination and the presidency. To accomplish this purpose, they mobilized the money power of the Wall Street bankers, the intellectual influences of the academic community - which is subservient to the wealth of the great tax-free foundations - and the media controllers represented in the membership of the CFR and the

Trilaterals."

It was President Carter who selected Paul Volcker as the Chairman of the Federal Reserve Board. He was a supporter of the one world government from the start, and to achieve this, he advocated the further destruction of the American economy, saying: "The standard of living of the average American has to decline... I don't think you can escape that."

In *The Shadows of Power,* James Perloff clearly shows Carter's true colors as a supporter of global tyranny, and an enemy of American sovereignty. He summarized Carter's attitude thus: "One is hard pi pressed to find major Carter foreign policy decisions that served the interests of the American people or the free world."

One of the goals of the Trilateral Commission and, in fact, the entire conspiracy, is to gain global power reducing the world's population through manufactured %rises" - like the 'overpopulation crisis," "the energy crisis," and "the agricultural crisis."

Manipulation of agriculture has always been a pet project of the conspiracy, because all humans have to eat to survive. If they can control agricultural production (or lack thereof), it is a relatively simple matter to induce famine (as in Ethiopia), riots and other unrest, or to persuade the population to knuckle under to their demands...

Many patriots fear - and rightly so - that the conspirators will use artificially-induced food shortages (which they create) to tighten controls over American citizens, taking away the last vestiges of rights and freedoms that we still have... especially the right to keep and bear arms, which is still protected by the Second Amendment to the Constitution. There have been numerous reports by federal employees of the secretive and highly classified stockpiling of enormous amounts of food in huge, secret underground vaults and storage areas! The questions arise: "Why are they stockpiling food?" and "Why all the secrecy? Why isn't the public informed of these colossal and well-stocked storage areas?" The answer is painfully obvious. These food stockpiles are not intended for the American citizens, in the event of a crisis. They are rather intended for the use of our new "masters," to help them survive the several massive "food shortages" which they have planned... They are counting on using the shortage of food as one of their 'aces in the hole', should the American citizens not submit docilely to the final surrender of our Constitution and national sovereignty to the New World Order Dictators... or in the event of a second American Revolution from the grassroots, level, before the New World Order has a chance to solidify their governmental structures.

You see, the conspirators are still very nervous about the fact that so many Americans still have guns - and they are having a very difficult time in getting control of all the guns out there. Short of descending on the American citizens with tanks and foreign troops (which they are already preparing for, under the guise of UN "peace-keeping" forces), what better way to seize control of all the privately-owned American guns, than to manufacture a severe food shortage? It would go something like this: "Hi! We're from your government. We're here to help. Do you want to eat? ... Then GIVE *US YOUR GUNS!!*" (When approached by the conspiracy through agents of President Roosevelt on the possibility of attacking the United States during World War 2, Hitler flatly refused, saying it would be too difficult and risky because of the number of private Americans who owned guns, which could not first be traced and confiscated!)

Control of U.S. agriculture with the ultimate intent of gaining the ability to create and manipulate food shortages for easy subjugation of the people has been a primary focus of the conspirators ever since the "reign" of FDR. For example, an article in the Arizona *Republic* of July 20th, 1992, states that the U.S. agricultural policy has been created with the purpose of destruction from the very beginning. The article reads:

"For 60 years the U.S. Department of Agriculture has waged war against increased farm production and lower food prices. Since the adoption of the Agriculture Adjustment Act in 1933 [our 'beloved' FDR works his evil once again!], the intent of the government's farm policy has been to organize scarcity... [If you don't believe this, then maybe you can answer why, during the blackest days of the Depression, when many Americans were literally starving in the streets, our benign and saintly President Franklin Roosevelt ordered untold countless tons of excellent, healthy crops and livestock be destroyed and 'plowed under,' so they could not be used by the starving American citizens who so desperately needed them... to 'stabilize food prices'...? Don't believe it!]

"What does this system of socialized farming mean for the average American consumer? Higher prices, of course... Total subsidies run between $10 billion and $20 billion. A free agricultural market would work if it were only given a chance!"

This article not only gives us insight into the plan of the conspirators to cause scarcity and higher costs in food, it also depicts the intentional wastefulness of bureaucrats to hasten the downfall of the Constitutional government.

This war on agriculture has been going on at least since the creation of the Federal Reserve. William Jennings Bryan explained the Agricultural Depression of 1920-2 1: "The Federal Reserve Bank that should have been the farmer's greatest protection has become his greatest foe. The deflation of the farmer was a crime deliberately committed."

The Trilateral Commission has been instrumental in implementing programs that prepare us for the last steps toward one world global socialism and totalitarianism. Thus far they have been very successful because of their influence with key people in the highest levels of our government (Bill Clinton is a member, as are most of the key people in his administration)... As Roy Ash, an insider in the Nixon administration said gloatingly on May 18th, 1972: "Within two decades the institutional framework for a World Economic Community will be in place... [when] aspects of individual sovereignty will be given over to supernational authority." He made that comment just over two decades ago... and, as it turns out, he was right!

In 1981, Congressman Larry McDonald took the matter of the Trilateral Commission's growing influence on government before Congress, calling for a comprehensive investigation of the CFR and the Commission in response to the American Legion Resolution 773, which urged Congress to investigate the influence these two organizations have on U.S. policy.

Despite no coverage from the establishment controlled media (what a surprise!), and having only limited success in Congress, McDonald would not give up, exposing the plot right up to the moment of his death aboard Korean Airlines 0077 in 1983... The conspiracy-planned downing of flight 0077 to silence an adversary of the CFR and Trilateral Commission brought a cry of vengeance from the state level. Again in spite of no media coverage, those aware of the conspiracy waged a behind-the-scenes battle to apply pressure on Congress to continue and intensify the investigation of the CFR and the Commission.

On April 3rd, 1985, the Indiana House of Representatives introduced Resolution 19, calling for further investigations. However, because of lack of public pressure and no media coverage, the resolution went unanswered! (How's that for " responsible government!" Responsible, yes... but to whom??!)

While many Congressmen decided to back off (undoubtedly fearing for their own lives), others, particularly Senator Jesse Helms, intensified their efforts to expose the plot to create a one-world government. Speaking before his colleagues on December 15, 1987, Senator Helms said,

"This campaign against the American people, against traditional American culture and values, is systematic psychological warfare. It is orchestrated by a vast array of interests comprising not only the Eastern establishment, but also the radical left. Among this group we find the Department of State, the Department of Commerce, the money center banks and multinational corporations, the media, the educational establishment, the entertainment industry, and the large tax-exempt foundations.

"Mr. President, a careful examination of what is happening behind the scenes reveals that all of these interests are working in concert with the masters of the Kremlin in order to create what some refer to as a New World Order. Private organizations such as the Council on Foreign Relations, the Royal Institute of International Affairs, and the Bilderberger group, among others, serve to disseminate and to coordinate the plans for this so-called new world order in powerful business, financial, academic, and official circles.

"The psychological campaign that I am describing is the work of groups within the Eastern establishment, that amorphous amalgam of wealth and social connections whose power resides in its control over our financial system and over a large portion of our industrial sector. The principal instrument of this control over the American economy and money is the Federal Reserve System. The policies of the industrial sectors, primarily the multinational corporations, are influenced by the money center banks through debt financing and through the large blocks of stock controlled by the trust departments of the money center banks.

"Anyone familiar with American history, and particularly American economic history, cannot fail to notice the control over the Department of State and the Central Intelligence Agency which Wall Street seems to exercise. The influence of establishment insiders over our foreign policy has become a fact of life in our time... The viewpoint of the establishment today is called globalism.' Not long ago, its critics did call this viewpoint the 'one world' view... "Mr. President, in the globalist point of view, nation-states and national boundaries do not count for anything... Indeed, even constitutions are irrelevant to the exercise of power... All that matters to this club is the maximization of profits resulting from the practice of what can be described as finance capitalism, a system that rests upon the twin pillars of debt and monopoly. It isn't real capitalism. It is the road to economic concentration and to political slavery."

1960-1990

"I believe there are more instances of the abridgement of the freedom of the people by gradual and silent encroachments of those in power than by violent and sudden usurpations. " - James Madison

Although the conspiracy-controlled media would have us believe otherwise, the domestic policy of the U.S. government for more than 60 years has been created, not with America's best interests, but with her total destruction in mind. Any attempt at reversing this trend was immediately and severely (often *permanently),* dealt with... For example: President Kennedy, although involved with the conspiracy since his initial rise to power, decided that enough was enough, and was planning to pull out of Vietnam, not to mention the fact that he signed executive order #11110 - which created silver backed certificates (U.S. Dollars). The conspiracy did not like either of these actions, so they killed him!

Lynne Meredith, in *Vultures In Eagles' Clothing* explains:

"On June 4th, 1963, via Executive Order #11110, authorized the issuance of $4 billion dollars in debt-free, unborrowed United States Notes (dollars)! These would have been United States Silver Certificates, *"redeemable in silver, against all silver bullion, silver, or standard silver dollars in the Treasury not then held for redemption of any outstanding silver certificates and to further coin standard silver dollars..."*

"Furthermore, in a chilling speech made to Columbia University, ten days before his assassination, Kennedy stated, 'the high office of the President has been used to foment a plot to destroy the Americans' freedom - and before I leave office, I must inform the Citizen of his plight!'"

On November 22nd, 1963, Kennedy was assassinated by Lee Harvey Oswald - a disenfranchised, confused, ex-U.S. soldier, who had already defected to the Soviet Union a few years earlier, and who was used by the conspiracy to stop Kennedy before he could do them real damage (Somehow, Timothy McVeigh - the alleged bomber of the April 19th, 1995, Oklahoma City tragedy - comes to mind!).

Lynne Meredith continues: "After Kennedy's assassination, one of the first Executive Orders of Lyndon Johnson, as the new president, was to rescind Kennedy's Executive Order #11110, and have the silver certificates that had already been printed, destroyed! Further serving as the voice of the Federal Reserve, Johnson told the American people that "silver has become too valuable to use as money.' (WHAT"?) Then on July 23rd, 1965, in an act as unlawful as FDR's gold robbery, Johnson signed a bill authorizing the issuance of copper clad coins to replace silver coins, and abolished all silver certificates!

"This action was a direct and blatant violation of Article 1, Section 10 of the Constitution, which states: "No State shall.. coin money, emit bills of credit, nor make anything but gold and silver coin a tender in payment of debts...""

"On the day of President Kennedy's funeral, the first 50 million Federal Reserve Notes which were "non-redeemable" in silver were released into circulation. Kennedy's Silver Certificates, and the prosperity they could have brought our nation were buried with Kennedy!

"What happened to all of that silver, that we American Citizens would have benefited from in the form of debt-free silver certificates? [It went straight to the pockets of - who else? - the international banking conspirators, of course! through their 'front men' in the Federal Reserve!] The Coinage Act of 1965, passed after Kennedy's assassination, provided: 'The Treasury is authorized to sell any silver in excess of that required to be held against outstanding "silver certificates," for $1.29 per troy ounce to the Federal Reserve!'"

Johnson also not only continued, but also dramatically upscaled the war in Vietnam... but he wasn't satisfied yet (or rather his puppet-masters in the international banking conspiracy were not yet satisfied)... He also initiated the "Great Society" program, saying, "We are going to take all the money we think is unnecessarily being spent, and take it from the 'haves', and give it to the 'have-nots' that need it so much."

Later President Nixon put the final nail in the coffin of the monetary system, by eliminating all ties between gold and the value of the dollar.

At the 1980 Republican convention, Senator Barry Goldwater said, "This might be the last Republican conventions, and in two weeks, the last Democratic convention, 'Mere are forces working against our country. They are selfish interests working against all Americans for their own gain."

Just prior to the 1980 election, Ronald Reagan said, "I think there is an elite in this country and they are the ones who run an elitist government. They want a government by a handful of people because they don't believe the people themselves can run their lives... Are we going to have an elitist government that makes decisions for people's lives, or are we going to believe as we have for so many decades, that the people can make these decisions for themselves?"

One of the major elements of the conspirators' plans is to completely collapse the economy of the U.S. through the banking interests, using both private and public debt. This is the reason the U.S. has gone deeper and deeper into debt and is blatantly wasteful. Although it is possible that some degree of wasteful spending could be due to ignorance, greed, and stupidity, it takes a purposeful effort to destroy such an enormous amount of wealth and create the mounds of debt that have accumulated under the government over the past few decades.

'My idea is to spend! Even if it is all waste! The conspirators didn't actually take all of our property and resources and throw them away, however. They haven't been wantonly squandering America's vast wealth... Far from it! They have instead stuffed it into their own pockets! And now it's payback time! We must first, however, inform our fellow citizens of the truth! Only then can we regain our country and our future! Remember: Exposure = death for the conspiracy!

Just to give you a better grasp of the enormity of the crime that the international banking conspirators have perpetrated against Americans, let's look at some figures. In 1960, the federal debt was $290 billion. By 1980 it was over I trillion... Today, as this report is being written, the debt is about $5 trillion! To put it another way, it took 198 years for the federal government to borrow the first trillions dollars. Then it took just 12 more years to increase the debt by an additional $3 trillion. Finally, in just two more years, the debt has grown by another $2 trillion... The worst of it is that the rate of increase keeps going higher and higher. Currently, the federal debt is skyrocketing by over one billion dollars *every* day! more than eleven thousand rive hundred dollars ($11,500) *every single second!!*

" Million, " "billion, " "trillion, " - they are all just words, and words are easy to toss around. What's harder to understand is exactly how huge these numbers really are! Let's draw a simple analogy to give you a better picture of how much money we're talking about.

Imagine that you are in a large room full of one-dollar bills, and it's your job to count it all. If the room contained only one million dollars and you counted one bill every second without stopping, it would take you over eleven and one-half days!!... And that's just one million! Now imagine that the room (it would actually have to be a huge building) contained one *billion* dollars. If you counted one bill every second without stopping - 24 hours a day, it would take you over thirty-one and one-half YEARS!!! And that's 'just' one billion! That's how much our so-called federal 'debt' is increasing *every day!* One trillion dollars would take almost thirty-one thousand seven hundred ten (31,710) years!! Multiply that times five, and you get 158,549.95 years! Get the picture? That's how much money these thieves claim we owe them!!...

If our banking system were as it should be, according to the Constitution, this would be exactly as if Congress requested the U.S. Mint to print - let's say, for the purpose of illustration - one billion dollars. Then, when the Mint delivers the money, it says, "Here's the billion dollars you wanted us to print for you. By the way, you now owe us this billion -plus *interest!* (Excuse me! They merely printed *our* money! Now, suddenly, it becomes a *their* money, which we 'borrowed' and have to pay back? I don't think so!)... Yet that is exactly what we (through our leadless fearers') are making us do! That's right! We are expected to pay back the Federal Reserve for *our own money - which we never 'borrowed' from them in the first place!* And, as if that weren't bad enough, they didn't even *print* the money for us! They simply requested the U.S. Mint to print it, just as

Congress is *supposed* to do... The United States government should merely request the treasury to print bills - and pay them for the printing only. How can we allow the Federal Reserve to merely request a print job, then tell us that our money is now theirs, which we have to pay back - plus *interest!* Are you getting angry, yet? I certainly *hope so!*

By 1992 interest on the national debt was- already consuming 57% of all the revenue collected by income tax. It is estimated that at the current rate, the interest will consume 100% of all collected revenues by 1998... and then, what?

Another interesting fact is that in 1992, for the first time, there were more people working for the government than for all of the manufacturing companies in the private sector! This means that there are more 'citizens' collecting checks from the government than paying income taxes!

The typical American now pays approximately 45% of his or her income in Federal taxes including social security. State, county, and local taxes increase the tax bite even more. This means that the average person now works more than half of the year for the government! As an article in the June, 1992 issue of *Consumer Reports* explains:

"The average U.S. household has maintained its living standard largely because families are working more hours. Millions of women entered the work force in the past 25 years. In 1970, about 21 million women worked full time. Now that figure is over 36 million. That has helped to keep the family buying power fairly stable. But for most families, it now represents the labor of two earners rather than one."

And this only pertains to families that have been able to maintain their living standard. In reality, the net standard of living of the average family has been falling dramatically for many years: The amount of leisure time has shrunk to less than half what it was just a little over twenty years ago! The number of people who own their own homes has dropped drastically... The age at which the average family acquires a first home is rising... In many areas, it has become almost impossible for a single person or a family with just one wage earner to be even able to move into an apartment! The middle class is shrinking in size as more and more families fall below the official poverty level... Personal bankruptcies are at an all-time high... Over 95% of all Americans are broke at age 65... Not a pretty picture!

As Paul Volcker, head of the Federal Reserve in 1979 said, "The standard of living of the average American has to decline... I don't think you can argue with that." (!) As the *Nation* newspaper so clearly put it in a December I 11th, 1982 article on the rising inflation and faltering U.S. economy: "The blame for all this lies at the door of the Federal Reserve System - working as usual on behalf of the international banking cartel."

G. Edward Griffin, in his insightful book on the Federal Reserve, explains how the conspirators have been systematically implementing the gradual yet total collapse of the U.S. a economy: "It is not stupidity that pays farmers to destroy their crops, or that purchases trillion-dollar weapons systems that are never deployed or in some case never even completed. The overriding object behind most of these boondoggles is to waste the resources of the nation. The decline in living standards in the Western world is not the result of a widening gap between the haves and the have-nots, as we are told. It is the result of a conscious plan to maintain and widen that gap. To that end, massive waste in government spending is not an unfortunate by-product... It is the GOAL!

The proof is all around us and it is becoming increasingly clearer every day... the economy of the U.S. - and in fact the economy of the entire world - is collapsing under the weight of the global conspirators economic tyranny. Obviously, none of this happened by accident! And it is equally obvious that this cannot go on much longer.

America is headed for complete bankruptcy, which is exactly what the conspirators want. As will be explained in the next section, a complete credit and currency crisis would allow them to initiate the final stages of their plan to submerge all of us into a global totalitarian government. Or, as Gaither of the Ford Foundation said, "To be comfortably merged with Russia."

The U.S.S.R. - Dead?... Wrong!

Never forget that the devil's cleverest trick is- to convince you that he does not exist. Baudelaire

After all the U.S.S.R. went through to achieve world communism, does it not seem strange that it went under without a fight? Are glasnost, perestroika, and the collapse of the Soviet Union for real - or are they just one more deception designed to lead us into the conspirators' trap of global tyranny?

Since the much-heralded 'collapse of the Soviet Union,' the United States has given and lent billions of dollars to Russia. Unfortunately, according to an article entitled "The Russian Sinkhole" by Leslie Gelb in the March 30th, 1992 issue of *The New York Times,* "the ex-Soviet states are now meeting only 30% of their interest payments (and no principle) on more than $70 billion in debts to the West. Various forms of Western aid to the ex-Soviets totaled about $50 billion in the last 20 months... and the money has virtually disappeared without a trace, or a dent in the economic picture."

This process of throwing money at Russia and the ex-Soviet Bloc has only accelerated in the past three years since the above article, yet the economy of Russia remains in shambles. It's hard to believe that more than $120 billion could go to the Russian economy without making a dent. The question arises: "Where does all the money go, if not to help the Russian people?"

Once again, this is all part of the conspirators' plot. They not only want to funnel American taxpayer money through Russia to line their pockets and serve their drive toward a global dictatorship, but they also wand to decrease the standard of living in the wealthy countries, so they can be merged into a one-world government quickly and easily.

Dimitri Manalusky, Soviet diplomat, said: "We will offer the Christian world unheard of peace overtures, and these nations, stupid and decadent, will leap at the chance to be our friends. They will willingly co-operate in their own destruction. Then, when their guard is down and they have gone to sleep, we will smash them with our clenched fist."

General Sir Walter Walker, former NATO commander-in-chief, said just after the break-up of the U.S.S.R.: "I consider it my duty to tell you of the extremely dangerous threats that lie ahead. I know for certain that we are now in a period of the greatest strategic deception, perhaps in all history... 'Me cold war is not over, only in a state of remission."

Soviet defector Anatoliy Golitsyn, has been able to predict with uncanny accuracy not only perestroika and glasnost, but also the so-called 'collapse' of the Soviet Union - which is reality nothing more than a very elaborate hoax, designed to throw the Western world off-guard, and to make us believe that we are traveling a new road toward peace and harmony... In reality the aim is the convergence of "Communism" and "Capitalism," so that the masters of the new-world order, who already completely control the communist bloc, can effortlessly take over the capitalist western nations (mainly the U.S. and Europe) as well, in the name of "harmony" and "progress."

On the surface, this sounds great: the emergence of a new world, free from national boundaries and national or racial tensions... much like the vision of earth in the ever-popular "Star Trek," or John Lennon's song, "Imagine." Unfortunately, the reality of such a convergence will be much less utopian... just as the ideals of Communism may have sounded benign and altruistic on paper, but in the real world were the embodiment of the worst tyrannical despotism the world has ever known.

Golitsyn, with his well-earned authority on the subject of Soviet (read that as 'the conspirators') oppression, states: "Convergence will be accompanied by blood baths and political re-education (i.e. 'concentration') camps in Western Europe and the United States. The [conspirators] are counting on an economic depression in the United States [which they will create and manipulate!], and intend to introduce their reformed model of socialism with a human face as a alternative to the American system during the depression [caused by the bankers]."

As William F. Jasper states in his article, "Deadly Deception - The Myth of the Collapse of Communism", in the September, 1995 issue of The New American: "The convergence strategy is already well on its way toward completion. A principle apostle of convergence, Mr. Gorbachev, has been given a prime piece of real estate [the 'Presidio' in San Francisco] for his 'foundation,' and is accorded the status of royalty. Soviet soldiers are being trained at our most advanced military bases by our elite forces. Soviet KGB officers are being welcomed into our police forces. Leading Soviet disinformation agents are given prime time to disgorge their slick 'human face' propaganda to American television audiences. "

The "human face" propaganda referred to means simply that the image of the former Soviet Union is no longer being presented as a ruthless, cold, tyrannical, military dictatorship, run by fierce, joyless, highly-disciplined, military officers. We are now being shown the very human side of the citizens of the former U.S.S.R. - We see them laughing, talking, crying, playing with their children, hugging their friends and family members, relishing their lives while struggling to survive... just like we do. This kind of imagery creates a great deal of empathy toward the very countries we were previously taught to regard as our enemies. But we must look past the propaganda, and realize that the people of these countries were always human beings - just as we are... and they were *never* our enemies. The fact is, the same tyrants have enslaved us both, and therefore, ironically enough, we have both been facing the same enemy all along! Our only enemy (and theirs) was - and still is - the international banking conspiracy!

William F. Jasper continues: "It is not the *reality of* the enemy, the *reality of* the threat, which is being eroded, but the *image* only; the threat remains, more real than ever. Diabolical? Certainly. The Communists [as puppets of the conspiracy] have ever shown their demonic capacity to mimic the deceptive techniques of the 'father of lies.' As the French poet Baudelaire admonished, 'Never forget that the devil's cleverest trick is to convince you that he does not exist.' Yes, he does exist, as do his demonic earthly minions who continue to use his deceitful wiles to spread their totalitarian empire across the globe under the rubric *of* the new world order."

Thought Control - Through the Media and Education

"The people never give up their liberties but under some delusion. Edmond Burke

Some people say that there is no way that a conspiracy of any magnitude could ever occur, because it would be discovered, or the public would get wind *of* it somehow. They would scoff at a report like this, and say that a conspiracy as big as we are talking about would have leaked out somehow. These people have fallen victim to the misinformation, half-truths, twisted facts, subtle innuendos, complete omissions, and outright lies of the conspiracy-control led media.

This may be hard to believe, but the conspiracy has

gradually gained total domination *of* all systems (media) of information communication, with the exception *of* private, self-publishers (like those who produced this report), and the Internet. They own controlling interests in all major radio and television networks and cable companies, all major movie studios, all major recording companies, all news wire services, all major newspapers and magazines, all major publishing companies (including those that publish "best sellers", dictionaries, history books, textbooks for all students from kindergarten through university, even children's books), all the major magazines and newspapers... in other words, practically everything we see, hear or read!

According to Congressman Oscar Callaway, the conspiracy's control of the media started in 1915 (while he was in Congress). Callaway made these comments on the Congressional Record: "In March, 1915, the J.P. Morgan interests got together 12 men high up in the newspaper world and employed them to select a sufficient number of the most influential newspapers in America, to control generally the policy of the daily press of the United States.

"These 12 men worked the problem out by selecting 179 newspapers, and then began by an elimination process to retain only those necessary for the purpose of controlling. They found it was only necessary to purchase control of 25 of the greatest papers... An editor was furnished for each paper, to properly supervise and edit information regarding the questions of political policies and other things of national and international nature considered vital to the interests of the purchasers." *[Congressional Record,* February 9th, 19171

In 1953, Harry Elmer Barnes, a noted historian, described how the censorship process works... "The methods followed by the various groups interested in blacking out the truth about world affairs since 1932 are numerous and ingenious. But, aside from subterranean persecution of individuals, they fall mainly into the following patterns or categories: 1) Excluding scholars suspected of revisionist [meaning opposed to the conspiracy-control led establishment] views from access to public documents which are freely opened to 'court historians', and other apologists for the foreign policy of President Franklin Roosevelt; 2) Intimidating publishers of books and periodicals, so that even those who might wish to publish books and articles setting forth the revisionist point of view, do not dare to do so; 3) Ignoring or obscuring published material which embodies revisionist facts and arguments; and 4) Smearing revisionist authors and their books.

"Leading members of the two largest publishing houses in the country have told me that, whatever their personal wishes in the circumstances, they would not feel it ethical to endanger their business and the property rights of their stockholders by publishing critical books relative to American foreign policy since 1933. And there is good reason for this hesitancy. The book clubs and the main sales outlets for books are controlled by powerful pressure groups, which are opposed to truth on such matters. These outlets not only refuse to market critical books in this field, but also threaten to boycott other books by those publishers who defy their blackout ultimatum." *[Perpetual War for Perpetual Peace,* Harry Elmer Barnes]

The depth of the control the conspiracy holds over the media, and the resulting media blackout of any news, publication or other information exposing the conspirators, is explained by Michael Parenti in his book, *Inventing Reality:*

"Ten business and financial cooperations control the three major television and radio networks (NBC, CBS, and ABC), 34 subsidiary television stations, 201 cable TV systems, 62 radio stations, 20 record companies, 59 magazines, 58 newspapers (including the *New York Times,* the

Washington Post, The Wall Street Journal, The Chicago Tribune, and the Los *Angeles Times),* 41 book publishers, and numerous motion picture companies like Columbia, MGM, Universal, Warner Brothers, and Twentieth Century Fox. Three quarters of the major stockholders of ABC, CBS, and NBC are banks, such as Chase Manhattan, Morgan Guaranty Trust, Citibank, and Bank of America.

"The overall pattern is one of increasing concentration of ownership and earnings. According to a 1982 Los *Angeles Times* survey, independent daily newspapers are being gobbled up by the chains at the rate of fifty or sixty a year. Ten newspaper chains earn over half of all newspaper revenue in this country. Five media conglomerates share 95% of the record and tapes market with Warner and CBS alone controlling 65% of the market. Eight Hollywood studios account for 89% of U.S. feature film rentals. Three television networks earn over two-thirds of total U.S. television revenues. Seven paperback publishers dominate the mass market for books.

"While having an abundance of numbers and giving an appearance of diversity, the mass media actually are highly centralized outlets that proffer a remarkably homogenized fare. News services for dailies throughout the entire nation are provided by the Associated Press and the United Press International, the New York Times-Washington Post Wire Services, and several foreign wire services like Reuters [all conspiracy controlled]. The ideological viewpoint of these news conduits are pretty much the same, marked by prefabricated standardization of news which is constricting and frightening."

Ben H. Bagdiklan in his book, *The Media Monopoly,* has this to say: "The power to control information is a major lever in the control of society. Giving citizens a choice in ideas and information is as important as giving them a choice in politics. If a nation has narrowly controlled information, it will soon have narrowly controlled politics."

At a meeting of the Independent Press in 1953, John Swinton, editor of the *New York Times,* said: "There is no such thing, at this date of the world's history, as an independent press. You know it and I know it. There is not one of you who dare write your honest opinions, and if you did, you know beforehand that it would never appear in print. I am paid weekly for keeping my honest opinions out of the paper I am connected with. Others of you are paid similar salaries for similar things, and any of you who would be so foolish as to write honest opinions would be out on the streets looking for another job. If I allowed my honest opinion to appear in one issue of my paper, before 24 hours had elapsed my occupation would be gone.

"The business of the journalist is to destroy the truth; to lie outright; to pervert; to vilify; to fawn at the feet of mammon; and to sell his country for his daily bread. You know it and I know it... and what folly is this - toasting an 'independent press'? We are the tools and vassals of the rich men behind the scenes. We are the jumping jacks. They pull the strings and we dance. Our talents, our possibilities and our lives are all the property of other men. We are intellectual prostitutes! "

Even David Rockefeller admitted the existence of a media conspiracy to further the conspirators' plans. In June of 1991, while giving a speech to the Bilderbergers in Baden Baden, Germany (at which he thought no one present would repeat what he said), he made the following statement: "We are grateful to the *Washington* Post, the *New York Times, Time Magazine,* and other great publications, whose directors have attended our meetings and respected their promise of discretion [silence] for almost forty years... It would have been impossible for us to develop our plan for the world if we had been subject to the bright lights of publicity during these years. But, the world is now more sophisticated and prepared to march towards a world government. The supranatural sovereignty of an intellectual elite and world bankers is surely preferable to national auto-determinational nation practiced in past centuries."

With the control of the media and information, the international banking conspirators have instituted another step in Amschel Rothschild's plan for global domination.

Education - or Brainwashing?

An equally sinister step in the plan to establish a new world order is the control of education - not only in America, but internationally...

The Rothschilds were the financial backers to Cecil Rhodes, who monopolized the gold and diamond industries of South Africa. (Cecil Rhodes - and therefore the Rothschilds - with the help of the British military, seized the wealth of South Africa from the native inhabitants through the Boer War!) Rhodes also dreamt of global domination, and must have felt right at home as an agent of the Rothschilds. Rhodes, in fact, wished to found an Order, which would serve as an instrument of the will of the Rothschild/Illuminati dynasty.

Rhodes' desire culminated with the founding of the "Rhodes Scholarship" program, to which he left his entire ill-gotten fortune after his death. As Carroll Quigley, author of *Tragedy and Hope,* explained: "The scholarships were merely a facade to conceal the secret society." The Rhodes foundation has always - from its very beginning to today - bestowed the honor of "Rhodes Scholar" on the best and brightest young minds, then systematically indoctrinated them into the utopian, one-world philosophies of the Illuminati/Rothschilds, in which the scholars would be members of the "enlightened", ruling class. (Remember: "Illuminati" means "enlightened ones!")

To this day, the Rhodes foundation is dedicated to a one-world government, which they promote to impressionable young minds as "benign" and "in the best interests of mankind." ... A case in point: Bill Clinton was a Rhodes scholar!

The Reece Committee, a committee convened to study the major U.S. foundations such as Carnegie, Ford, Rhodes, Rockefeller, etc., stated that the evidence compiled during the investigation "leads one to the conclusion that there was, indeed, something in the nature of an actual conspiracy among certain leading educators in the United States to bring about Socialism through the use of our school systems. This movement was heavily financed by leading foundations."

Congressman Eugene Cox confirmed: "The Rockefeller Foundation's funds have been used to finance individuals an organizations whose business it has been to get communism into the private and public schools of this country."

Without control of the school system, the control of the media would not have been as effective. Therefore, control of the schools was absolutely necessary. Hitler pointed out the effectiveness of controlling the schools systems: "When an opponent declares, 'I will not come over to your side,' I calmly say, 'your child belongs to us already. What are you? You will pass on. Your descendants, however, now stand in the new camp. In a short time they will know nothing else but this new community.'"

Undoubtedly, the government has accepted all of the ideas on schooling the international banking conspirators endorse. For example, in 1969, the Commission of Mental Health and Children (funded by the government) issued a report, which stated: "The school system, as the major socializing agency in the community, must assume a direct responsibility for the attitudes and values of child development." In-the Commission's (i.e. government's) eyes, no longer were the community, church, or even the parents responsible for the socialization of children. It was now the responsibility of the state... just like in Hitler's Germany or the Soviet Union!

This control of the school systems has become so pervasive and blatant that the National Education Association wrote in one of their reports: "Schools will become clinics whose purpose is to provide individualized, psycho-social treatment for the student, and teachers must become psycho-social therapists." This will include biochemical and psychological mediation of learning, as drugs are introduced experimentally to "improve" in the learner such qualities as personality, concentration and memory... As Phyllis Schafly commented: "Children are to become the objects of experimentation."

In 1973, Dr. Medford Evans, a researcher on the education system in America, summed up the state of "education" when he said: "Government schools make it a matter of policy to spend as much money as possible, and to impart as little knowledge as possible, since spending money imparts power, while keeping the scholars ignorant monopolizes power in the hands of the government insiders."

But what possible reason could they have for "keeping the scholars ignorant?" Isn't conditioning students into accepting the system (brainwashing) their entire reason for gaining control of education? True. But "Conditioning" does not include "imparting knowledge" - quite to the contrary. As Dr. Benjamin Rush observed in 1786: "Freedom can exist only in a society of knowledge. Without learning, men are incapable of knowing their rights. " Or, as the saying goes, "If you don't know your rights, you don't have any!"

According to an article in the May 30th, 1977, issue of *American Opinion:* "The only way to maintain control of the population was to obtain control of education in the U.S. They realized this was a prodigious task, so they approached the Rockefeller Foundation with the suggestion that they form in tandem - that portion of education which could be considered as domestically oriented be taken over by the Rockefeller Foundation, and that portion which was oriented to international matters be taken over by the Carnegie Endowment.

TODAY

"They are now on page 16 of The Plan... A British insider

From history, we may conclude that a nation or a people can be conquered by any one of five methods: war, religion, political ideology, legal conquest, or economic conquest. The international banking conspiracy, in order to assure itself of victory over the American people, has used not merely one, but all five methods to conquer the United States!

- They have instigated and manipulated war for profit and power.

- They have banned all religious teachings and prayer from public schools. They have branded the free expression of Christian beliefs as "politically incorrect," (free expression of other religious beliefs is still acceptable - as it should be for all religions, including Christianity). They have erased all Christian holidays from calendars sold to the public or used in schools, except those most easily exploited for profit: Christmas; Easter; and "All Hallow's Eve" (now known as "Halloween"), which is the night before the November 1st celebration of "All Saints' Day"... The original significance of those holidays have been thoroughly corrupted, distorted, or obliterated entirely. Holidays of other religions are still published on calendars - just as they should be, and just as Christian holidays should also be, out of fairness to everyone.

- They have brainwashed us into believing that we have a "democracy" - which is really no more than mob rule -

instead of a "Republic" - which is government by duly elected representatives (we don't pledge allegiance "...to the 'democracy' for which it stands...", nor do we sing "The Battle Hymn of the 'Democracy'"). They have also used the political ideology of "liberalism" to brainwash us into acceptance of socialism (which is just another word for "communism).

- They have changed the legal system from Common Law to statutory or admiralty (martial) law... Under Common Law (or the laws of nature), we are Sovereigns - superior to our servant, the government - and "endowed by our Creator with certain unalienable rights," (which are enumerated in and protected by the Constitution). Under statutory law, we are inferior to our 'master,' the government - which grants us "civil" rights and "privileges," that the government can (and does) take away whenever it wants!

- They have seized total control of our money, devaluing it beyond recognition, while stealing all of our gold, silver, and other property; and purposely plunged us into a so-called "debt" so enormous, that we can never hope to pay it off even if we sold all the land and personal property in the entire country ten times over!

After reviewing all of the facts and quotations contained in this report, I'm sure you have no doubt that today America is indeed a "conquered nation" - even though most Americans are still blissfully unaware of just how serious our plight is! ... Still, the conspirators have much work to do before they can bury without hope of resurrection, "the land of the free, and the home of the brave." They are very aware of this fact, and are working diligently to hammer the last nails into the coffin of American sovereignty and liberty! And therein lies our only hope for the future of our country - and, in fact, of the entire world!

We must spread the truth about what these criminals - these *thieves and murderers - have done to us, as well as what they are ultimately planning to do, as quickly as we can to our fellow Americans, and to our families, friends, colleagues, and associates in other countries (who are also victims at the hands of the criminal international banking conspiracy, and who will also suffer the same fate that is in store for us)... Remember.- Exposure = Death to the Conspiracy!*

But if enough people don't become aware of what is happening, we can expect the following (much of which has already happened!) to occur within the next 5 years or less:

1) The National ID Card

There has been much speculation as to what form the biblical prophecy of the "sign of the beast" will appear... Some think it will be the implantation of microchips into the skin (hand?) of all "slaves" to the conspiracy. Others discuss the possibility of implementing "debit cards," which are much like today's credit cards, but carry all personal history of the card-holder in the electronic strip already familiar to credit card holders... But it now seems more likely that the "sign of the beast" will be the already emerging "national ID card," which is being introduced to the general population in driver's licenses! Initially, this "national ID card" will be supposedly to eliminate "illegal aliens" from working in this country, when, in fact, the real reason will be to obtain instant access to personal information such as name, address, phone number, social security number (which was intended all along to be a national ID number), bank accounts (including access codes and account balances!), medical history, spending habits, outstanding bills, tax information, etc.

This "National ID Card" will no doubt be foisted on the unsuspecting American citizenry as a so-called "protection against illegal immigration... As Ralph Epperson, author *of The Unseen Hand,* explains: "So now the American people can begin to understand why the United States government is not doing more to prohibit the immigration of millions of 'illegal aliens.'" The truth is, the conspirators (through the federal government), are actually encouraging illegal aliens to enter the country, by giving them unemployment compensation, health care, free education, and other benefits - while forcing American citizens to pick up the tab (as usual)!

If you doubt this, just ask Californians about *Proposition 187* - which refuses illegal aliens all of these taxpayer-funded benefits... A recent supreme court decision overturned this proposition, saying essentially that American citizens have no right to refuse to pay (!) for all *of* the benefits and hand-outs the federal government promises to all illegal aliens!" Most Californians themselves don't "qualify" for these massive government (taxpayer) give-aways! The only possible reason for this travesty is to encourage as many people as possible to enter the country illegally! Why? So "they" (the government) will have an excuse to create more "controls" in order to stop this "crisis" which they themselves instigated!

They will then claim that the "National ID Card" would serve as a "right-to-work" card, identifying Americans as "Citizens *of* the United States" (meaning citizen of - and therefore subject to - the Federal Government). But that is not the real reason behind the push toward creating a "National ID Card."

The Arizona Star of March 25th, 1981, carried an article with the following headline: "Senator Dennis DeConci [Democrat from Arizona at that time] 'Not Averse' to National Worker ID to Curb Alien Influx." The article went on to say that a national registration of all people would not be out of the question - supposedly to curb "the tremendous benefits of coming over here illegally." Of course, this rationale is strictly for public consumption...

The <u>real </u>reason for creating this card - which is already experimentally in effect in many parts of the country - would be to have total access to all information regarding any individual. "Who cares?" you might ask. "I have nothing to hide." Well, it isn't about hiding anything... it's about being able to effectively, and quietly control any individuals who are considered 'dangerous' or 'unfriendly' to the "Establishment" of the impending New World Order... This would include not only private citizens, but also religious, civil and political leaders, as well as duly elected officials. The international banking conspiracy, with the help of puppets and co-conspirators in our government (most notably Jimmy Carter, who created FEMA; and Bill Clinton, who unlawfully gave the UN power to decide who enters U.S.), have already created the necessary machinery and facilities to incarcerate 'unruly' citizens and officials!

2) The MJTF

The "Multi-Jurisdictional Task Force" (MJTF) is a horrifying example of 'Big Brother', closing in on the innocent population. It consists of local police, county sheriffs, state National Guard units, federal law enforcement agencies, and UN 'peace keeping' forces -all under federal/UN control. Their purpose is to conduct house-to-house search and seizure raids on American citizens, and to operate the detention centers for 'unruly citizens' [meaning 'citizens who refuse to be ruled'], under FEMA (Federal Emergency Management Association).

To assist them in their police-state actions against any of their 'slaves' (American citizens) who refuse to be docile servants to the New World Order, they have the Orwellian technology of the Treasury Enforcement Communications System (TECS) already set up and at their command! (If you still think these guys have your best interests at heart, just ask yourself: "Why does the Treasury need any form of 'enforcement?'"... "What kind of 'enforcement?'" - and "Against whom?"... The answer is obvious: "To force us to remain in their illegal money system (based on debt instead of real value), and thereby maintain absolute control over us while siphoning off the profits from our productivity to line their parasitical pockets!")

The TECS links telecommunication terminals located in offices of enforcement agencies across the United States, with similar 'enforcement communication systems' throughout the world to the international banking conspiracy's huge and sophisticated central computer terminal in Brussels, Belgium. The TECS system accommodates the IRS/BATF, Customs, Immigration, the Drug Enforcement Agency (DEA), the State Department, the Justice Department, the Coast Guard, and Interpol. TECS can tap into every existing major database from automobile registration files to credit reporting agencies and county and local files (including bank accounts, telephone records, drivers licenses, marriage and business licenses, traffic violations, birth, and death certificates, and everything else 'of public record!') NOTHING is left untouched, or out of their reach!

Through the use of this (TECS) system, based upon mere suspicion, they can start tracking you, and watch your every move! The manner in which it is used gives no weight or value to your personal rights to liberty, property, or privacy!

3) UN "Peacekeeping" Forces

About now, you're probably wondering, "How will these so-called 'unruly citizens' (which could - and will - be anyone who opposes the new global dictatorship) be 'contained'...? Simple. Enter the already ubiquitous UN 'peace-keeping' forces... The clincher is that there will be no actual American soldiers involved in the "quelling of political unrest" right here in our own back yards. Instead, we will be looking down the wrong end of a gun barrel, in the hands of a soldier from another country, who will not have as many reservations about pulling the trigger as a soldier who just happens to be a fellow American citizen might! If you don't believe me, just ask the citizens of Bosnia, who had to stare into guns held by soldiers from the United States - or other 'foreign countries!'... The soldier would be simply 'doing his duty,' which includes regarding the local citizens as 'the enemy,' whom he has already been ordered to fire upon, if necessary! It is a well-documented fact (although studiously ignored by the conspiracy-controlled media) that the United States is already over-run with foreign troops!

But what about our own American boys (and girls) who are part of the occupying forces in foreign countries against whom we have no quarrel and have declared no war? What about them? - Our own soldiers, who have been instructed (by the conspirators, under the so-called 'peace-keeping' mission of the UN) to fire upon innocent civilians of other countries?? Do you think our own soldiers would have as many misgivings about firing into a crowd of foreign civilians on foreign soil as he/she would have about firing into a crowd of Americans on American soil? - I don't think so!

4) Federal Emergency Management Agency (FEMA)

Howard Freeman, a leading researcher and speaker in the patriot movement, tells of a chance visit he had with the governor of Wyoming in 1991: "He is very concerned that if he runs for office this November [1992], that there won't be a State of Wyoming at the end of four years. He believes that the International Bankers might foreclose on the nation and officially admit that they own the whole world. They could round up everybody in the State Capitol building, put them in an interment camp and hold them indefinitely. They may give them a trial, or they may not. They will do whatever they want. As I explained earlier, it has not been expedient to foreclose on the nation until they could get everything ready. This is where the Federal Emergency Management Agency (FEMA) comes in. It has been put in place without anyone really noticing it.

"FEMA has been designed for when America is officially declared bankrupt, which would be a national emergency. In a national emergency, all Constitutional Rights and all law that previously existed would be suspended. FEMA has created large concentration camps where they would put anyone who might cause trouble for the orderly plan and process of the new regime to take over the nation. [According to Jack Lamb in *Vampire Killer 2000,* the L.A. riots were instigated as a test run for the installment of FEMA!)

"Even a governor could be thrown into one of these internment camps, and kept there indefinitely. This is all in place now, and they are just waiting to declare a national emergency. Then, even state governments could be dissolved. Anybody who might oppose the new regime could be imprisoned until a new set of laws could be implemented and a new government set up. The Governor [of Wyoming] knows all this, and he is very concerned. He doesn't want to be in office when all this happens."

President Jimmy Carter created FEMA by Executive Order in 1978. This organization is a *civilian agency,* with authority to administer a totalitarian government in the event of domestic or international crisis. FEMA has the authority to:

"Relocate millions of workers, reorganize national industry and banking, and distribute all economic resources and transportation access; operate every level of government, through personnel currently in place throughout Washington and the rest of the country; institute total energy rationing; and order mass evacuation of residents in the perimeter of nuclear power plants." ("FEMA: Your Emergency Government in the Wings?" *Fusion* magazine, August, 1980)

5) Constitutional Convention

When America was founded, the Rothschilds and their international banking conspiracy were very unhappy because it was founded on the Common Law. The Common Law is based on *substance - or* things that are 'real' (like the original United States Dollars, which were backed by gold and silver), as opposed to things that are 'colorable' (like the Federal Reserve Notes, which are backed by nothing. According to Black's Law Dictionary, the word "colorable" is defined as: "That which is in appearance only, and not in reality, what it purports to be, hence counterfeit, feigned, having the appearance of truth." Therefore, Federal Reserve Notes are actually counterfeit dollars, not real dollars!

(... Just in case you were wondering, Black's Law Dictionary is the 'bible' used by our 'statutory' courts to re-define words of common English usage in such a way as to trick people outside the legal profession into entrapping themselves, by admitting that they are subject to the federal government, and therefore 'liable' to pay taxes, obtain licenses for 'permission' - granted to them by their new master, the federal government - for common, everyday activities - such as being born, getting married, working, driving a car, dying, etc.)

Even though the conspirators have had 100% success in stealing all of our property along with most of our rights, and have nearly succeeded in plunging us into a world-wide dictatorship, they are worried - Big Time! There is a growing grassroots patriot movement to reclaim our country and return to the Constitution, real dollars (backed by substance such as gold and silver), and Common Law. The conspirators know that since the Constitution still stands (even though for the most part it has been circumvented), citizens still have the ability to "wake up," reclaim their own sovereignty, and stand on Common Law, refusing to be used as a slave by the federal government...

exactly as hundreds of thousands of Americans have already done!

Don't get me wrong, the conspiracy is not concerned over a handful of "dissidents," which it can (and does) effectively smear through its propaganda machine, the media, by labeling them as "crackpots," "extremists," "radicals,

"isolationists," "hate mongers," "separatists," etc. What really has the conspirators worried is the fact that, with the

Constitution still in place, their power is not "absolute" - the American people still have "a way out" which the conspirators cannot deny without exposing not only their criminal actions, but also their ultimate plan!

To eliminate this potential danger of exposure, and to push America closer to the world dictatorship, in early 1995, the conspirators tried to organize a "Conference of the States" (COS), which in reality was nothing more than an attempt to convene a second "constitutional convention," with the sole purpose of radically altering the Constitution of the United States, instituting a "transitional Congress," which would dissolve the individual state governments, and install a nationwide "party" system (does the U.S.S.R. ring a bell?), while totally eliminating the American citizens' individual sovereignty... This attempt at changing the Constitution was de defeated because the grassroots patriot movement effectively mobilized enough citizens to petition their state governments to reject participation in the COS, and the subsequent radical, conspiracy-written changes to our Constitution.

If nothing more, you should have at least learned from this report that the conspirators never give up. They are still planning to organize another constitutional convention, which they could refer to as a "Conference of States," "Council of State Governments" (CGS), or some other name... But as long as our Constitution exists in tact, they are still forced to recognize our rights as sovereigns over them! Be aware, however, that once the United States is placed under the UN as a "member state" of the world government, our Constitution will be automatically nullified under the UN "Covenant" as will all other national constitutions and charters.

6) Currency Collapse

One of the last steps the conspiracy is planning for the United States be ore they dictatorship implement their world dictatorship will be the total collapse of the "dollar" (which is already counterfeit and completely without any real value). They will do this in order to "make public" the fact that the United States government is bankrupt (which it has already been for more than 60 years!)... By introducing this "problem" of bankruptcy (which they created!), the conspiracy will then be in the position to offer their "solution" (which they also created)... that of introducing a "new 'dollar'" which will be even more worthless than the current "dollar" (thus providing them with yet another chance to steal wealth from the American people!)... This new dollar - just like the German Mark and Mexican Peso before it - will be worth only a fraction of what the old "dollar" was worth...

There is no way of predicting exactly how much the new "dollar" will be "worth," but - just to give you an idea of the possibilities - at this writing, the "dollar" is hovering at around 1/400 per ounce of gold (or gold is now "worth" approximately $400 an ounce). Insider sources indicate that very soon (within the next few years at the latest), gold will be worth approximately $5,000 (five thousand dollars) an ounce! This would effectively make our new dollars worth *less than one-tenth of* their current value!! Imagine! A loaf of bread or a carton of milk will cost $20... but (and here is the real "clincher") the people will still be earning the same amount of "dollars" as before the currency collapse!

For your information, the "new 'dollars" have already been printed - several billion "dollars" worth - and are just waiting in the Federal Reserve storage vaults for release! According to Carl Mintz, on the staff *of* the House Banking Committee, "I believe it's in the billions of dollars, and it's buried in lots of places." This duplicate currency will remain buried, unissued, and virtually unknown until confidence in the present "dollar" is completely shattered... These new dollars will be known as "blue chip dollars" because the one-dollar bills are blue. The other dollar amounts are various other colors.

To make the change in currency easier for the American public to accept, the Federal Reserve has already announced a series of "facelifts" for the present Federal Reserve Notes, which are to be introduced gradually over a period of several years. The purpose of these "facelifts" is supposedly to deter counterfeiting - but the *real* reason is to condition Americans to accept changes in the appearance of the dollar. At this is writing, the first of the dollar " facelifts " has already ready been introduced with the new 100 dollar bill, on which there is a larger, slightly off-center portrait of Benjamin Franklin. Watch for more "facelifts" on bills of other denominations, which will follow soon.

7) Gun Control

The chief stumbling block for the conspirators' establishment of their world dictatorship has always been the American citizen's "right to keep and bear arms," which is protected by the Second Amendment to the Constitution. Although they have managed to severely limit and regulate our right to "bear arms," they have not been able to completely do away with our right to have those arms in the first place - although they have been industriously chipping away at our right to "keep arms" by ever increasing regulations and registration requirements... (It's interesting to note that the Gun Control Act of 1968 was taken - WORD FOR WORD from a Nazi Germany gun law! ...

Hmmm!)

One of the key tactics of the conspirators has always been to create a "problem" or "crisis", and then to offer a "solution" through legislation and regulations. They have been vigorously applying this tactic to disarm the American people by touting "anti-crime" legislation in such a way as to make it seem that if normal citizens give up their guns (which is our last line of defense and one of the only things keeping the conspirators from initiating their final plan), then crime will be reduced. This is an obvious absurdity! The government actually encourages crime because it gives greater impetus for 11 gun control," and because crime keeps the population subdued.

As Eustace Mullins explains in his excellent book, *The World Order,* "The Federal Government uses its armed police, the IRS, the FBI, the BATF, and the CIA solely to terrorize its American subjects into compliance with the program of the World Order. They [the American public] now realize that the IRS functions as an armed group of terrorists, not to collect funds, of which the government has no need, but solely to extort money by force from American citizens, as part of the program of the World Order."

A confidential study done by the conspiracy's own Club of Rome in 1985 estimated that there are between 200 to 250 million guns in the hands of private American citizens! It also estimated that 10% of the population would rise up against the establishment of a police state/new world order. 'Me Club of Rome report also estimated that it would only take 5% of the population to stop the implementation of such a dictatorship!

The patriot movement (meaning those American citizens who are aware of what is happening and want to stop it by returning to government under our Constitution) has been estimated to be anywhere from 20 to 40 million strong, and growing rapidly! ... This would give us a 5% to 10% margin of safety already. Many of those in the patriot movement (which merely means those who have learned the truth and do not want to be a part of the world dictatorship) do not even own guns themselves! The "gun owners" are for the most part hunters, sportsmen/women, hobbyists, ranchers, and many who live in rural areas, among others. They are (by and large) not even in the patriot movement (but probably would be if they learned the truth!)... So, you see, the conspirators have good reason to be concerned. They genuinely fear a general uprising before they have a chance to implement their world dictatorship, and they are becoming desperate!

How desperate? Ask the victims of the government slaughter at the Branch Davidian Compound in Waco, Texas what their "crime" was to justify the gassing and burning of 80 people (including 25 children) who were minding their own business. Ask them why the government laid relentless siege to them for 51 days before subjecting them all to a horrifying nightmare of death, without so much as a trial, a hearing, or even a warrant! They can't answer now, but we can. The government (read that as "conspirators") knew they had guns (as protected under the Second Amendment), and feared they might instigate an uprising (even though there was absolutely no evidence of this alleged intent on the part of the Davidians). The government claimed, "child abuse" (again without evidence) - so to justify its actions, it approved the mass murder of 25 children to prevent them from being abused? GIVE ME A BREAK!

Ask Randy Weaver of Ruby Ridge, Idaho, why his 14 year old son, Sammy, and his wife, Vicki, were murdered by the conspiracy-controlled FBI... Sammy and a family friend were walking with the aging family dog one morning, when an FBI agent brutally shot the dog dead at Sammy's feet, while following his superior's orders: "First, we have to take out the dog." When Sammy turned to run home to safety, he was shot twice: the first shot ripped off his arm;

the second shot (in the back) killed him. Sammy had done nothing wrong. He was just a kid! But that wasn't enough for the conspirators' thugs. The next day, Randy's wife, Vicki, was shot through the head while she stood - unarmed - in the doorway of their home, their 10-month-old baby daughter in her arms! What was Randy's crime to merit such a brutal attack on his family? He sold a shotgun to a conspiracy insider who had badgered him for 3 years to purchase the weapon... In reality, the conspiracy was out to silence Randy, (whom they branded as a "white separatist" - a blatant lie!) for speaking out against the international banking conspiracy on numerous occasions to local residents.

Ask Edye Smith, whose two young children (Chase, age 3 and Colton, age 2), were killed in the tragic Oklahoma City bombing, why the top officials of the ATF (the IRS's enforcement arm, the Bureau of Alcohol, Tobacco, and Firearms) "just happened" to be out of their offices in the Alfred P. Murray Federal Office Building on April 19th, 1995...

According to Edye, "We, along with hundreds of thousands of other people, want to know, where was the ATF the morning of April 19th? All of their employees survived, they were supposed to be the target or this explosion and where were they? They were given the option of not going to work that day. We just want to know *why*, and they're telling us, "Keep your mouth shut. Don't talk about it!" ...An ATF agent who *was* in the building but survived was asked, "How did you get out of there alive?" To the disbelief of those listening, he responded, "I don't know what's going on. I *got a page yesterday, on my beeper, and was told* not to come to work today!" ... Gee! What a coincidence! (!!!)

Isn't it also an interesting coincidence that the Clinton administration "just happened" to have been unsuccessfully trying to ram a controversial " Anti-Terrorist Act" through Congress just before the tragic bombing incident? (Opponents to this Act, insist that it would not help to deter terrorism, but would do a great deal to further destroy American citizens' right to privacy, and to "keep and bear arms!") And even more interesting coincidence is that the Anti-Terrorist Act "just happened" to gain tremendous momentum directly as a result of this bombing, with the media fanning the flames of the public outrage over the senseless and brutal act -especially concerning the tragic deaths of the young children in the day care center...

The most amazing "coincidence" of all is that there "just happened" to be a bomb squad parked in the parking lot of the Murray building in the morning of April 19th, as noticed by many people arriving at work between 7:00 and 9:00 AM!!

The Clinton administration wasted no time in accusing the patriot movement of this horrible crime, and lambasted anyone who speaks out against the government, hinting that they are "unpatriotic," or "potential terrorists" who should be punished for their "un-American" views (under the Anti-Terrorist Act, perhaps?)... But they also ordered the building destroyed before a full investigation could reveal any more evidence. Numerous independent explosives experts have since concurred that there was actually a *second* blast - targeted *directly at the day-care center (!) - which* did the actual damage. This is contrary to the conspirators'"media" propaganda, which credits destruction to the pathetic homemade device delivered by the truck allegedly driven by Timothy McVeigh (whom thoughtful observers believe to be an obvious 1. patsy," planted by the conspiracy to place the blame on the patriot movement)!

8) Government "Spying" on Citizens Through Massive Simultaneous Wiretap - *It is the opinion of this writer (and practically everyone else who has found out what is *really*

going on) that the AntiTerrorist Act was aimed directly at the American citizens, so the government could label anyone they felt opposed their ill-gotten power or the coming world dictatorship as an "enemy." It was also intended to provide the federal government with an excuse to enact extensive new spying powers on the citizens...

For instance, a recent order by the justice department, directed all telephone companies to add electronic wiretap capability to all telephone lines! In addition, the entire United States was ordered into the web of caller ID by the end of 1995! This means every time you make a call, the telephone line also automatically transmits your name, your address, and your telephone number, making telephone privacy a thing of the past (unless you obtain a device to block the automatic ID)! By October of 1998, telephone companies must reach "capacity" requirements to handle the huge volume potential of their ubiquitous wiretap equipment already in place, to make their equipment capable of supporting federal eavesdropping on a massive scale of up to 1.5 million simultaneous wiretaps on Americans! If that doesn't scare you (and make you furious), then nothing will! Unless, of course it's:

9) Weather "Mod modification"/Control

Weather control/modification is a hush-hush subject insofar as the conspiracy-controlled media is concerned... But what better way to destroy an enemy's capacity to make war than with bad weather? As impossible and ridiculous as this sounds, the fact is, the governments of both the United States and the U.S.S.R. worked (largely in conjunction) for years on technology to harness the vast forces of nature. The end purpose of this research and development was not to create harsh weather conditions as a means of thwarting advancing armies or deterring insurrections. NO, the purpose was much more sinister and dangerous than that. It was designed to be used as a transportation system for biological warfare!

As retired Colonel Donn Grand Pre revealed in an article appearing in the July 31st, 1995 issue of "The Spotlight" newspaper, entitled *Weather Modification Could Become Top Weapon:* "Yes, we have a weapon in our arsenal, as do the ex-Soviets, so devastating that it could nullify every other weapon extant today. It is called weather modification. Used selectively with the vast stock-piles of biological agents located in the United States, in the ex-U.S.S.R. and in Israel, it could wipe out -or at the very least incapacitate - every person in a target area as vast as half the continent of Africa!"

10) The State of New Columbia

In 1990, Washington D.C. seceded from the United States! It is now officially called "the State of New Columbia," and has its own flag, and a "constitution" which places it directly under control of the United Nations and the UN Covenant! As if that weren't bad enough, President Clinton is implementing a program in the public primary schools that have the young children pledging allegiance to the United Nations and the UN Flag!!! Naturally, there was/is a total media blackout on these horrifying acts of treason!

Why??

I doubt that anyone who has read this report will be able to dispute the fact that American citizens have been the victims of a hideous plot to rob them of their freedom, rights and privacy - and even their very dignity as human beings by the international banking conspiracy... So we know what happened, but it is much more difficult to understand why...

As far as the conspirators themselves, their motives were/are clear - to create a world dictatorship with them at the top as the "ruling class," and the rest of us (including the entire population of the planet) as their "slaves. " -But what about the others who helped further the international banking conspiracy's plan for world dictatorship? The "little guys" who even though they knew what the plan was - went along with it without much hope of personal gain on their part?

I don't think I will ever understand how so many of our own fellow citizens who, being merely in some public capacity and not in line for the real "plumbs" of victory which the insiders in the conspiracy promised to their most powerful coconspirators in our government, still sold out their fellow citizens and the future of our country for - in most cases - not even a nod of thanks or glimmer of recognition (I'm referring mainly to politicians on the local and state levels as well as government workers, policemen, accountants, attorneys, and all varieties of establishment-pandering "gutless wonders."

I'm sorry, Patrick Henry, but maybe for these timid souls life is so sweet and peace is so dear as to be purchased at the price of chains and slavery... as long as they are not the ones who have to suffer!

Perhaps this is best expressed by Senator John Danforth from Missouri, as reported in the Arizona *Republic* of April 2 21st, 1992: "1 have never seen more senators express discontent with their jobs... I think the major cause is that, deep down in our hearts; we have been accomplices to doing something unforgivable to this wonderful country. Deep down in our hearts, we know that we have bankrupted America and that we have given our children a legacy of bankruptcy... We have defrauded our country to get elected."

... In the words of Alan Stag, author of Taxscam, "We have lost our country... The only question worth asking now is:

'How do we get it back?'"

A NEW BEGINNING

Hopefully, this report has silenced any doubts that you may have had about the existence of the conspiracy, and along with those doubts, any urge you may have previously held (as carefully nurtured in us all by the conspiracy/establishment controlled media) to scoff at 'conspiracy theories.' Because now is the time to take action! - But I don't mean that you should run out into the streets to instigate a revolution... far from it! You need only take action in your own life by extracting yourself from "the system" and declaring your own freedom! This is the only way you will be able to realize an immediate and positive effect on not only your own life (of which you have always been the 'Master,' no matter what others may tell you!), and in so doing, begin to influence positively the lives of others with whom you come into contact on a regular basis...

As you 'take action' in your own life, keep in mind that you will face great opposition - not so much from the conspiracy/establishment, but from your own friends and relatives. You will hear ridiculous things - like, "You will get into trouble!" "You will go to jail!"; "You can go ahead and break the 'law' if you want to, but I'll have no part of it!"; "You won't drag me down with you!"... Please remember that they are speaking out of *ignorance of the facts!* They are speaking out of the brainwashed mindset that has been carefully instilled in all of us for more than 60 years! ... They are speaking out of fear... and maybe even out of envy that they don't have the same courage to stand up and claim their own freedom as guaranteed us by our forefathers under the Constitution!

Do not try to "convert" others - especially your own friends and family - into believing in their own personal power and right to their own lives! Simply show them by your own example - and possibly give (or lend) them a copy of this report... they will come around to the truth in their own time

- if they want to! Meanwhile, concentrate on getting this report into the hands of your own customers, or as many others as possible, who have expressed interest in taking back their own lives, and living under the 'Common Law' of Nature/God, as protected under our Constitution!

The opposition that your friends/family might express to you, is rooted in the fear that they *will* be subjugated to some sort of 'punishment' by the conspiracy (read that as "government") under the "Statutory 'Laws'" that we are supposed to obey. You need to understand that the "establishment/government/conspiracy" will NEVER EVEN TRY to prosecute you, because they know - much better than most of the rest of us - that THEY HAVEN'T GOT A LEG TO STAND ON! they *know* they are breaking the law (they are just hoping that you won't rind out)!!

Oh, sure, they may bluster a bit, but don't let it scare you... because, not only are you right - but also you now have a HUGE network of supporters who will leap to your defense - and send the rascals running for cover... which they don't have! ... If it makes you feel any better, there are common law courts, jury associations, and literally HUNDREDS of support groups springing up like wild flowers after a storm - all across the country! These patriot organizations are fighting back by suing the offending policemen, judges, IRS agents, and other 'co-conspirators' - and *winning!*

Before we go into details of what you can do - right *now - to* take back your life, your privacy, your rights and your freedom, I would like to share with you a true "Profile in Courage" which should serve as an inspiration to us all:

A Soldier Fights For His Country

"I am not a UN soldier.' - Army Specialist Michael New

A good soldier is trained to follow orders - even if it means killing another human... After all, it's their job! Even if our country has not actually declared war against the victims (such as in the "conflicts" of Korea, Viet Nam, El Salvador,

Panama, Grenada, Desert Storm, Haiti, Bosnia, etc.).

In all of these so-called "conflicts," our soldiers have bravely risked their lives following the orders of their commanding officers, because it is their sworn duty to serve in the United States Armed Forces... But now, our military is being deployed, not as "U.S. troops," but as "UN troops!" They are being asked to don UN uniforms, and to serve under foreign commanders! ... Even though the U.S. taxpayers are still picking up the bill - of course! I don't know about you, but I strongly disagree with this arrangement! As if it weren't bad enough that our military is being used for so-called "peace keeping" (read that as "Gestapo") duty, they are now being asked to risk their lives for a foreign power (the UN), in a brazen display of the conspiracy controlled UN's aspirations toward global dictatorship! So far, our troops have been meekly going along with the unauthorized change in their status from U.S. soldier (defender of the Constitution), to UN soldier (defender of the UN Charter)... except for one brave patriot who has challenged the UN orders, Michael New.

In a sensational act that scandalized the military, and was studiously ignored by the media, Army specialist Michael New, a decorated medic, flatly refused to don a UN uniform or wear UN insignia when he learned in August, 1995, that his unit, stationed in Germany, was to be deployed in Macedonia as part of a UN "peacekeeping" contingent in which American soldiers are required to wear UN insignia and serve under a foreign commander. When New expressed his willingness to serve with his buddies, but his unwillingness to wear the uniform of a foreign power he was informed by his superiors that he may face a court-martial for "disobeying a legal order."

New tried to explain his position to his lieutenant, saying, "Sir, I don't think I should have to wear a UN arm band or a UN beret. I'm enlisted in the U.S. army; I am not a UN soldier. I have taken no vow to the UN; I have taken an oath to defend the Constitution of the United States of America from enemies foreign and domestic. I regard the UN as a separate power... Where does my oath say that I have to wear UN insignia?"

The oath of service that New and all U.S. military take includes a pledge to "support and defend the Constitution of the United States against all enemies, foreign and domestic [and bear truth faith and allegiance to the same... without any mental reservation or purpose of evasion, so help me God." On the other hand, the UN's oath of service requires the affiant "to discharge those functions and regulate my conduct with the interests of the United Nations only in view [!], and not to seek or accept instructions in respect to the performance of my duties from any government or any other authority external to the organization."

New's parents inquired of Army Chief of Staff, General Dennis Reimer: "Are we to understand that the U.S. Army has I mental reservations,' or some 'purpose of evasion' when it administers the oath of service to soldiers? By what authority can the U.S. Army transfer my son's allegiance without his permission?"

Mrs. G.E. Coey, the mother of John Coey, a young medic who died in Rhodesia fighting communism, supports Michael New's "gallant stand to defend our United States Constitution and to resist tyranny."

Before his death in July, 1975, Coey wrote home to his parents the following insightful observation: "The enemy that threatens the West most... is not the terrorist, the street or campus revolutionary, the Viet Cong, or even the Soviets with their alleged nuclear arsenal, but the international conspiracy that has made and sustained communism. This is an enemy that usurps power, corrupts and controls governments, monetary and educational systems and the news media..."

John Coey's words show that there were soldiers in the U.S. military even 20 years ago who understood who the real enemy was... and Michael New's brave stand against the UN prove that there still are U.S. soldiers willing to uphold their oath to "support and defend the Constitution of the United States against all enemies foreign and domestic."

Michael New was court martialed and dishonorably discharged... His only "crime" was his strict adherence to the oath he swore when he joined the Army! It would seem that the international banking conspiracy is intent on treating patriotism as treason under the new world order!

Think of it! Now you can "spread the word" and help take our country back, and be paid for your efforts, by selling this report! Once again, thank you for ordering this important information! In closing, I'd like to leave you with a couple of poignant quotations which eloquently reflect the awakening spirit of men and women across this great land of ours!